Ethical Copywriting

Ethical Copywriting

A practical guide for coaches, healers, and service-based entrepreneurs to sell without the sleaze

Lauren Van Mullem

Copyright © 2025 by Lauren Van Mullem

All rights reserved. No part of this publication may be reproduced, distributed or transmitted in any form or by any means, including photocopying, recording, or other electronic or mechanical methods, without the prior written permission of the publisher, except in the case of brief quotations embodied in critical reviews and certain other noncommercial uses permitted by copyright law.

Every effort has been made to obtain permissions for materials quoted throughout the book. If any required acknowledgements have been omitted, or any rights overlooked, it is unintentional. Please notify the publisher of any omission, and it will be rectified in future editions.

Headshot Photography: Charles Modica Jr.

For permission requests, write to the author at: Lauren@truerwordsbylauren.com

Lauren Van Mullem
Ethical Copywriting / Lauren Van Mullem —1st ed.

EPUB: 978-1-956989-53-3

Dedication

This book is dedicated to caring copywriters and values-driven entrepreneurs who inwardly cringe at selling, wholeheartedly want to be of service, and *also* need to build sustainable, profitable businesses.

I promise:

You can be true to who you are and what you value while having a thriving business.

In fact, I believe it's necessary.

Fit Check

Let's make sure this book is a fit for you before you read any further. (Ethical copywriting, Step 1: Don't waste people's time if they're not a fit.)

This book is <u>NOT</u> for you if:
1. You already absolutely know what is right and what is wrong, black and white are your favorite colors, and you have zero patience for shades of gray.
2. You expect me to tell you what is right and wrong and think *I* should have all the answers. Anyone claiming to know all the answers is probably leading a cult. This book is here to help you find your own answers and make informed decisions about what copywriting and marketing practices feel right to you.
3. You firmly believe Ethics Are Serious Business and we shouldn't make jokes in their presence. You will find humor in this book. Can't guarantee it'll be good humor, but it's my humor.
4. You long for an in-depth exploration of anti-racism, anti-capitalism, decolonization, misogyny, ableism, global economics, geopolitics, and carbon footprints. Yay! Let's be friends! We are going to enter those waters, but you won't find a deep dive here because there is so much to be said on those topics (and not all of it by this well-meaning white lady). My expertise is in ethical

copywriting, so that is my focus. Working with those issues in mind is part of ethical copywriting, but each topic deserves a book (or several) of its own. I've listed my favorite resources for further study in the back of this book and in the footnotes throughout.

This book IS for you if:
1. You are a **service-based business owner** and probably a solopreneur wearing all or most of the hats for your business. This book is not written for product-based businesses.
2. You know in your heart that selling your services with mainstream marketing tactics feels icky and wrong, and you're searching for another way to make your business work. You want someone to say, "This way! This works!" This book will help you find your way to articulate what you do and share it with clients who can't wait to work with you. While I can't guarantee results, these methods work better over time—to bring in right-fit clients—than manipulative, coercive "conversion" tactics focused solely on client acquisition.
3. You're into practical solutions you can use right now, not just ideas. While you'll find both here, I'm excited to show you how to put the ideas of ethical marketing into practice when writing for your business.
4. You want results like:
    a. More right-fit clients who want what you offer, love what you deliver, and can't wait to tell everyone about you.
    b. Higher completion rates for your courses and programs (part of the magic of basing your sales

practices on establishing fit).
c. Clients who are actively invested in their success and don't expect you to wave your wand and make their lives perfect.
d. Fewer wrong-fit clients who make you question every life choice that led you to entrepreneurship. You'll learn how to build an almost-perfect filter.
e. A freebie that prospective clients actually engage with, rather than download, save to their desktop, and forget because *who has time to read another freebie?*
f. Emails that get read AND responded to by your highly engaged list who thinks of you as a trusted friend.

If that sounds like you, read on.

"Over the past few millennia, writing has become a craft, every bit as noble as making clothing, pottery, or a magnificent timber frame hall. And craft is the thing. If you are thinking of reading this book, then you have a craft—perhaps as a coach or healer of some kind—but there's a secondary craft of how to write about it, how to put the arcane mysteries, felt-senses, unarticulated intuitions and inklings into words that your ideal client would read and say, 'That's me!'

They say that if you play one string on a violin, that same string on another violin will begin to vibrate in resonance. Words can do that too. Words become the adornments you wear that cause the eyes of your perfect customer to light up and lean in. You've poured your heart into building the home of your business but the words are the paint and wallpaper, the hanging plants and old lamps that bring it to life. It's possible to write about your business in a way that affirms that deep spirit of a people who've forgotten how to be a people (the ethos) and that gets you the right clients (the marketing).

Lauren Van Mullem, better than most I know, can show you how to take the beautiful woven fabric of your business and tailor stitch it into bespoke, tailor-made clothes that have your dream clients say 'hello.'"

TAD HARGRAVE,
FOUNDER, MARKETING FOR HIPPIES

Contents

Dedication v
Fit Check vii
Introduction 1

Chapter 1   Welcome to the Wild West 9
Chapter 2   Getting Clear on Your Values 15
Chapter 3   Getting Clear on Your VALUE 27
Chapter 4   Charm, Pain, and the Lizard Brain 35
Chapter 5   How to Write a Non-Icky Sales Page 53
Chapter 6   How to Talk About Yourself (and Why You Should) 91
Chapter 7   Not-So-Free Freebies and Other Thinly Veiled Sales Pitches 111
Chapter 8   Emails That Get Read (and Not Because of Clickbait Titles) 127
Chapter 9   Social Media Done Dirty 151
Chapter 10   Conscious Word Choice 161
Chapter 11   AI Copy—Yes, No, It Depends? 169

Conclusion 189
Resources 191
Gratitude 193

Introduction

This is a book about how to clearly articulate who you are as a business owner and what you do for your clients so your people can find you—and recognize that you have what they need.

This is also a book about how *not* to do that.

If you're reading this, you are already painfully aware that marketing and sales feel icky, smarmy, and—deep down—kinda *wrong*. But you've been told that icky-feeling marketing tactics are the only way to get clients and build your business to sustain yourself and your family without stepping into someone else's office again.

Many entrepreneurs are willing to do <u>anything</u> for the promise of money and freedom.

You're here because you aren't willing to do *anything*. For you, the ends don't justify the means. But you don't know what to do instead (that will work). I believe that the means are equally important to the ends—and how you choose to write the marketing copy for your business can set you apart so even *more* people want to work with you.

The numbers

Thirty percent of Millennials and 29% of Gen Zers say sharing values and ethics with brands is *more important than price* when deciding to buy—and that is across industries, from buying ethically made, PFAS free underwear to purchasing programs from trusted coaches and influencers.[1] But when you are a service-based solopreneur, the importance of shared values is even more crucial. When someone chooses to work with you, they are inviting you into their lives and investing time and money in your promises, which is a vulnerable position. This requires so much trust.

Studies show that when consumers don't trust a company—specifically because they perceive it as unethical—consumer satisfaction and loyalty plummet.[2] When you consider that copywriting is at the heart of nearly every communication you have at every touchpoint with your clients, ensuring your copy feels ethical and trustworthy has significant implications for profitability.

Profitability isn't the only metric to judge whether ethical marketing "works." It also works because it's easier for us, as conscious business owners, not to compromise our values. The cognitive load of forcing ourselves to "sell" using inauthentic systems quickly leads to dreading marketing tasks. So many of my clients tell me, "I hate marketing," and this dissonance is always why.

It can be simple...

If *mainstream* marketing's purpose is to make sales, *ethical* marketing's goal is for business owners and clients to benefit equally. For that to happen, ethical marketing must first establish a fit between what prospective clients need or want and what the business delivers.

---

[1] "2024 Global Consumer Trends Index." *Marigold, with EConsultancy*, January 2024.
[2] Leonidou, L.C., Kvasova, O., Leonidou, C.N. *et al.* Business Unethicality as an Impediment to Consumer Trust: The Moderating Role of Demographic and Cultural Characteristics. *J Bus Ethics* 112, 397–415 (2013). https://doi.org/10.1007/s10551-012-1267-9

Ethical marketing can be this simple:
> Can you deliver what your ideal clients need in the way they need it? Yes? Can you communicate that effectively? Yes = sale!
>
> No = NOT coercing them into a sale *you want* that doesn't serve them.

But that doesn't mean you should throw out everything you know about buyer psychology—how and why humans choose to buy. Knowing how the human mind works helps you communicate more clearly, with more empathy and care, delivering the information your clients need intellectually *and* emotionally so they can make the best decision. And consciously stop short of using that information to influence them toward your goals.

Remember: You do not have a right to anyone's time or money, even though so much of mainstream marketing assumes you do.

It can also be scary to be an outlier

I know what you're thinking: "What if I lose clients by not using the manipulative tactics everyone else uses?" Truthfully, you may lose a few clients in the short-term by not using manipulative sales tactics because those clients are not a good fit or it really isn't the right time for them to invest. This is a good thing. Because when you try to attract and convert everybody, including wrong-fit clients, they will be unhappy with your program, course, service, or product, and they will make your life a living hell. I'm talking about bad reviews, trashing your online reputation, bringing their angry energy to your group calls, and demanding more of your time than you're prepared to give as they try to make your offer work for them (when it was never going to work well). If I can't appeal to your altruism, let me appeal to your self-interest. Doing well by doing good is better for everyone.

You might also wonder if ethical marketing even applies to certain high-pressure industries, like insurance, finance, tech, fitness coaching, timeshares, car sales, or high-ticket coaching. I'll be honest with you: If your business model depends on selling a product or service one time to a lot of people, manipulative tactics may yield more sales. But if your business model depends on repeat clients, customer loyalty, long-term relationships, and referrals, you need marketing that nurtures those relationships. You can only do that sustainably by building trust and acting with integrity.

That's what this book is about.

Your first lesson: Question everything, including me.

Who the heck am I to be talking to you about ethical copywriting?

I am an ethical copywriter for coaches. Who gave me that title? Me. I did. It's not like there's a certification program or anything (at least not yet). One day, I decided I wouldn't write sales copy that felt icky anymore and then I figured out techniques that worked even better. That's the *Reader's Digest* summary. Now, make yourself a big mug of tea, because here's the unabridged version.

HOW I REACHED MY BREAKING POINT

In 2017, I was just scratching the glass ceiling of the six-figure income I always thought I wanted. I was working nonstop, going to the gym five days a week, stress-shopping on Etsy, and driving myself straight into burnout.

For nearly ten years, I'd worked in software-as-a-service (aka

SaaS, aka tech industry) as a content writer (read: glorified blogger) and copywriter. My specialty was ghostwriting thought-leadership content about customer-success best practices.

For those blessedly uninitiated into tech jargon: I wrote about how tech companies could help their customers reach their goals more effectively…and (because ghostwriting) my clients got authorship credit. I didn't mind that part. Good ghostwriters are responsible for sharing some of humanity's best stories. (Shout out to Prince Harry's ghostwriter—*Spare* was a real page-turner.)

What I did mind was writing for tech companies. The tech company folks I knew really were trying to help their clients solve problems and reach desired outcomes. They were all about making processes faster, easier, more streamlined, and more intuitive so people could be more productive.[3]

But I also saw companies paying lip service to making a positive impact on their customers while using psychologically manipulative, coercive tactics on their landing pages, emails, ads, and in the apps themselves.

I didn't hear anyone talking about another way to sell. We didn't know of one.

After nine years, I could not give a crap about another app. I couldn't even pretend to care. I was exhausted by the jargon, the hypocrisy, the "high-speed, agile" teams with highly motivated people in startups that would fold in six months. Then, my primary client hit burnout with a side of mental health crisis, and my income disappeared. Deep in burnout myself, I snapped.

I decided to quit EVERYTHING. *Privilege check!* My spouse, who

---

3   Author's opinion: Even if your app does help someone cram more to-dos into their overcrowded day, you're just driving them into burnout faster to prop up a flawed capitalist system. Ask me how I know. I've been to burnout land a LOT. (Recommended reading: *Rest Is Resistance* by Tricia Hersey.)

has been "patron of the arts" more than once over my career (read: supporting my broke ass), makes enough money for us to keep a roof over our heads whether I work or not. No frills or fun stuff, but a roof in Southern California ain't nothing. So I *could* quit. Theoretically.

I thought I might make hats, or become a painter, or be the most eccentric housewife ever. Cue identity crisis (how would I introduce myself at parties?!) and a heaping dose of culturally inculcated capitalist shame. If I didn't have a job title, who was I?

True to form, I avoided answering those big questions by distracting myself. Two weeks into unemployment, I received an email that read, "I've been wanting to work with you for so long, and I'm finally ready. Would you take on this one job?" That email was from a coach. And so was the next one.

By 2019, I was all in. I made a list of my absolute favorite clients from ten years of freelance writing, and they were almost all coaches. Life coaches, health coaches, spiritual coaches—the kind of folks who'd want to meet me over Zoom so they could check out my aura and vet me with their spirit guides. That was my new niche, which was entirely different from my SaaS background. None of my old contacts worked. The reputation I'd worked to build for ten years? That only counted in tech. I needed to rebrand and rebuild my business from scratch.

That's when I really started to question EVERYTHING.

See, the thing about SaaS is that it's on the "bleeding edge" of marketing strategy—that's their term. Not cutting edge. *Bleeding*. Tech industry copywriters are fueled by tracking data and A/B testing everything. The best ones have learned copywriting best practices from the 1930s to the *Mad Men*-era 1960s and continually test new ways to manipulate subconscious minds into taking action. Pain-pointy sales page intros are the tip of the iceberg.

That was my background when I switched my niche to coaches in

2019. I knew all the psychology tricks and how to test and *iterate* to make sure those tricks worked as effectively as possible—and I didn't want to do any of it.

But what else was there? At that time, no copywriting schools taught any other way. Ethical marketing wasn't on the radar.

So, I returned to what I'd always done best: telling people's stories, highlighting what made them different, and translating the emotional heart of their experiences into words that emotionally connected with their audiences.

It worked. It felt good, AND it worked.

Over time, I honed my philosophy about why some copywriting techniques felt good and others felt icky. I learned to identify tactics designed to trick the lizard brain into acting faster (such as pain points and countdown timers). And I developed clever swaps and replacements, questioning, dismantling, and putting pieces back together to create something I'd never been taught: a way to write and sell that felt generous, service-oriented, and ethical.

In this book, I'm not just going to teach you my favorite swaps and replacements for icky tactics and how to get to the heart of your story (you'll definitely learn that!). I will also encourage you to question everything so you can find answers that align with your values.

My goal is for you to use your creativity and critical thinking to expand the conversation about ethical marketing.

To be clear: I am not the authority on what is right or wrong.

I don't have a degree in philosophy. I've never taken an ethics class. To my knowledge, I am not a deity (despite what I tell my husband). I'm just a human trying to do right by my fellow humans.

If that's where you are, let's explore what that looks like together.

CHAPTER 1

Welcome to the Wild West

I'm going to break one of my own rules and ask you to "imagine if…"[4]

Imagine a world where every business respected your intelligence and treated you like a capable adult. No scarcity tactics. No countdown timers. No digging into your deepest insecurities (or manufacturing new ones for you) to sell products you don't need. Service offers and products would be created with the highest good in mind, using ethical labor and environmentally friendly materials. Influencers would present unfiltered bodies and messy kitchen counters. Coaches would be upfront about how hard it is and how long it takes to make lasting positive change. And we'd all feel a whole lot better about ourselves. Maybe we'd all even feel like we are enough and have enough.

Capitalism would inevitably crumble or transform into something extraordinary, maybe a gifting economy.[5]

I know this sounds impossible, and it probably is. But I believe ethical marketing can make consumers expect and demand better treatment. This future has a chance, and we're the ones who can tip the scales.

---

[4] Hi, have we met? Here's what you need to know about me: I'm Lauren, ethical copywriter, and I hate the words "imagine if" more than any other words in the English language. Even more than "moist." I'll get into my reasons later, don't you worry.

[5] Thanks, Robin Wall Kimmerer, for planting that seed in my mind with *The Serviceberry*.

But right now, we live in the Wild West, where business owners, business coaches, and marketers make up their own rules, and there is no sheriff around. Nobody is telling you that you have to market your business ethically. And even if they were, there are no standards or guidelines. It's not like "organic," where you can apply for a certification from the USDA that says you've followed particular practices and protocols. We don't even have a concrete definition of the phrase, just the individual words.

The *Oxford English Dictionary* definitions:
Ethical (adjective): connected with beliefs and principles about what is right and wrong.
Marketing (noun): the activity or business of promoting and selling products or services, including market research and advertising.[6]

Well, *that's* wide open to interpretation.

I'm not here to tell you what is right and wrong. I don't have that kind of authority—only you do. So, your first exercise is to think critically about what you believe is right, wrong, or "it depends."

I'll tell you how I make these calls myself, but the decision is yours. This book will give you a framework for how to think about the words you use on your website and in sales emails so your marketing communications feel right and good *to you*. And bring in clients who feel right and good too.

For these reasons, I'm not going to get into discussions about the nature of good and evil, the definition of right and wrong, or anything else better left to philosophers, academics, spiritual leaders,

---

6   The first known use of the word "marketing" was in 1561, from T. Norton Calvin's Inst. IV. xviii. 148 "How filthy markettinges they use, how unhonest gaines they make wt their massinges."

and pedants. *Can any form of marketing be ethical? Isn't all communication inherently manipulative?* Cool questions—let me know what answers you come to.

So, what is ethical copywriting?

All of the advice in this book is based on my definition of ethical copywriting:

Copy that gives consumers the information they need to make fully informed (and never coerced) decisions in their own best time.

This means no psychologically manipulative tactics that trick or pressure your brain into making a decision faster or differently than you would if you had all of the information, time, and resources.

"Copy" encompasses all written words used at any stage of the sales process—in ads, on websites, in emails, and in other written communications between businesses and their customers.

I am a copywriter, and this book is focused entirely on the words you write when your goal is to attract paying clients (also known as "sales copy"). You won't find business strategy, branding, design, SEO, or advice on content (like blog posts or Medium articles), though when discussing ethical marketing, we touch on all of those. But my scope is small.

In this book, you'll learn how to write about your work in a way that informs and clarifies in order to sell rather than compel. At its core, ethical copywriting is about establishing fit and value so your ideal clients immediately know if you and your solution are right for them.

You'll also learn to:
- Choose words to empathize with tender spots rather than to dig into pain points to trigger faster action.
- Support your ideal client's decision-making process, giving their rational mind what it needs to make wise choices rather than leveraging their lizard brain's fight/flight/freeze/appease instincts to avoid pain and react to fear.
- Use levels of awareness to inform your readers and give them an "aha" moment that leads to a sale…and, possibly, to the kind of awareness that fuels real social change.

Our focus here is on how to articulate the value of what you offer, who you are, the experience of working with you, and how your approach is different (and more effective) than what your ideal clients have already tried. Because when right-fit clients have all that information, they can make a fully informed decision about whether or not to hire you. The sale should happen naturally and enthusiastically. Without needing to push. Without even having to ask for it.

But here's the best part: When you start empowering people this way, they'll expect to be treated as rational, reasonable, intelligent humans capable of making their own decisions by <u>all businesses</u>. What an incredible world that would be. Let's make it happen.

Takeaways

1. **Define your ethics**: There's no universal standard for ethical marketing. So reflect on your beliefs about what is right, wrong, or situational. Trust your gut, especially when "experts" tell you something that feels off. In Chapter 2, we'll go deep into values, the core beliefs that guide your actions and attitudes, so you can define the ethics that guide your behavior.
2. **Focus on clarity and fit**: Write to clarify your offer, experience, and unique approach so ideal clients can easily recognize if you're the right fit. Ethical copywriting is about establishing that right fit between what you offer, how you offer it, and your ideal client who needs it. Don't worry about not being a "fit" for everyone—that's the point. You'll find this in every chapter because clarity and fit are that important. One thing you absolutely must get clear on is the value you bring to your clients, which we'll cover in Chapter 3.
3. **Avoid manipulation**: Reject tactics that exploit pain points, fear, or subconscious triggers to coerce decisions. Chapter 4 will be all about spotting these tactics, learning how they work, and how you can consciously subvert them without sacrificing effective marketing.
4. **Empower consumer decisions**: Ethical copywriting provides clients with all the facts they need to make informed, unpressured choices on their timelines. In Chapter 5, I'll show you how to do this step by step on a sales page.
5. **Lead by example**: Empowering your audience fosters a culture where businesses respect clients as rational, intelligent decision-makers. Be a pioneer for this change.

Before we move on to the next chapter, ask yourself: What marketing practices have felt icky to you? Start making a list as they come to mind because we'll be working with them (and against them) in the following pages.

CHAPTER 2

Getting Clear on Your Values

When I sent a newsletter reacting to the 2024 U.S. election results and talking about how I was putting my feminist rage into action, I got many enthusiastic replies, but one stood out: "Oh, I'm so glad you said this. I was thinking about working with you but wasn't sure where you stood. I'm filling out the form to book a call with you right now."

Values are the core beliefs that guide your actions and opinions on what is fair, just, good, and desirable. They're what you want for yourself and for other people. And when you apply them to your business, they are an incredibly powerful filtering tool to attract like-minded clients you'll immediately click with...and repel the rest.

Stating your values publicly makes your clients feel comfortable, safe, and good about working with you, which makes them more likely to buy from you and refer you to others. Research from 5W Public Relations in 2020 showed that 71% of consumers prefer buying from companies aligned with their values. The preference was even stronger among millennials, with 83% saying that sharing values with businesses was important when deciding to buy.[7]

---

7   5W Public Relations, *2020 Consumer Culture Report* (New York: 5W Public Relations, 2020). Data collected via online survey conducted from November 13 to 18, 2019, among a nationally representative sample of 1,001 American adults aged 18 and older.

Values not only sell—they contribute to the sustainability of your business because working with clients who agree with you on the important things is easier, more energizing, and more fun.

Let's look at where and how to talk about your values for your business.

Create a values page

When I wrote my website, I included a values page. The link to this page is in the footer, a tiny thing you might not see unless you look for it. It's mostly there for me. In my personal life, I have many values, like honesty, generosity, courage, compassion, and rebelliousness.[8] But for my website, I chose three values that guide my *business*: accessibility, people before profit, and inclusivity.

VALUES		
Accessibility	**People Before Profit**	**Inclusivity**
I want every business owner to have access to effective copywriting at accessible prices. For that reason, I specialize in offering DIY support, workbooks, and workshops.	"Put the person before the sale" means that your best interest comes first. I will not manipulate you for my benefit (or for your benefit—no manipulation, PERIOD).	I am deeply committed to working for accessibility, equality, equity, diversity, and full inclusion for Black, Brown, Indigenous, minority ethnic, people of color and LGBTQ+ communities.

---

8   I also have a simple moral code that I repeat to myself regularly. It goes like this. #1 Don't be an asshole. #2 Don't be a dumbass. #3 Don't be oversensitive. #4 Always use a coaster. I'm convinced it's the recipe for living life right.

This is a short page on purpose. You don't want to overwhelm your reader by listing all of your values, so make sure to pare your list down to essentials. A good place to start this process is with an old-fashioned brainstorming session.

Identifying your values

When you think about which values will guide your business, here are a few questions to consider:
1. What values would you like other businesses to have?
2. How would you want to be treated as a client/consumer if the situation were reversed?
3. If you're going to "be the change you want to see in the world" (thanks, Gandhi), what would that mean?
4. How do you want your ideal clients to feel when they first visit your website?
5. How do you want your clients to feel while working with you? And after?

Often, the seeds of your values were planted a long time ago by culture, spirituality, family, or injustices you experienced or witnessed. As you narrow down your list, it may help to think back to when each one became important to you and what emotions you've attached to the memory. Your clients likely have similar emotions and past experiences, which will make them feel seen and understood when they see your values page.

Another approach to zeroing in on your business values is to look at your personal values, what you prioritize in your daily life, and what principles guide your biggest decisions. I realize I'm flying in the face of an established paradigm that life and work are separate spheres. I've never been that good at compartmentalizing, and I'm not sure it's healthy or desirable to think of your business as separate from yourself. It seems to lead to denying responsibility and care for each other, of the "I just denied your healthcare claims, but it's *just business*" variety. But when you infuse your business with your personal values and treat it as an extension of how you care for people in your everyday life, that becomes a very different paradigm of the relationship between life and work. It's also the foundation of an authentic brand clients will rally behind.

Your values are one of your best differentiators in that people will choose to work with you because of your values. It's not just a moral compass—it's a strategic advantage.

Here is a short list of values to help you identify your own.

Accessibility	Equality	Learning
Accountability	Fairness	Making a difference
Altruism	Faith	Nature
Ambition	Freedom	Openness
Authenticity	Generosity	People before profit
Balance	Giving back	Reliability
Belonging	Gratitude	Responsibility
Caring	Growth	Self-respect
Commitment	Honesty	Service
Community	Hope	Simplicity
Compassion	Inclusivity	Spirituality
Courage	Integrity	Stewardship
Creativity	Intuition	Trust
Curiosity	Kindness	Truth
Diversity	Leadership	Vulnerability
Environment	Love	Wholeheartedness

Example time: how my values-driven business works

When a prospective client finds me online, I want to make sure they feel welcome and valued (inclusivity!). One of the ways I do that is to post testimonials from diverse clients on my website so people can see others like themselves and feel reassured that they've found a safe and welcoming place. I also acknowledge the gift inherent in my clients allowing me to use their testimonials this way—it's deeply generous of them and not something I take lightly.

For my value of accessibility, I never wanted anyone to look at my services and feel like they couldn't get help because they couldn't afford it. I grew up with a lot of financial uncertainty in a small town packed with wealthy people, and I know how much it hurts to see some people get everything they need to succeed when you have to make it work with fewer resources. So, even though clients and colleagues have told me for years to "raise your rates!" I've structured my business to support DIYers who are willing and able to put in the work to make their copy just as effective (if not more) than if they spent thousands on a "high-ticket" copywriter. Interestingly, I'm not making less by charging less. As my business model evolves more toward workbooks, workshops, and teaching, more people are able to work with me or do the work themselves, which means I'm making slightly more money than if I only worked with "high-ticket" clients, and I have more reach and impact to promote ethical copywriting.

Finally, when I think of putting people before profit, I think of radical generosity and transparency. As a consumer, I don't want to be treated like a transaction rather than a person. I want to feel cared for beyond the bounds of a contract. And I want to know the whole truth, upfront, with all of the information so that I can make the best decision for me. For that reason, I build generosity into both my paid and free offers, and I always make prices, dates, and other essential facts easy to find on my sales pages.

I know what you're thinking: "But does all of this get clients?" Here is an excerpt from an email sent by a prospect inquiring about my full-service offers:

> "I actually discovered you a couple of months ago and really resonated with you. I would love to collaborate with you, a copywriter and person who resonates with myself and the ethos of my business."

I receive messages like this *all the time*.

Living my values in my business isn't all rainbows and sausages. Sometimes my values demand I make hard choices, including turning down partnerships with business owners who use tactics I cannot endorse. When an opportunity to partner with a business owner or course creator arises, I have a vetting process that starts with me telling them, point blank, "I am an ethical copywriter, here's what that means. If that's not your style, I understand. We're probably not the best fit." If that doesn't scare them away, it really is the beginning of a beautiful, long, and lucrative relationship.

Questions to consider as you refine your values:
1. What are you willing to take a stand for? Or against?
2. What would you never, ever do?
3. What do you believe everyone should do (and wouldn't the world be better if they did)?

Values in action

Once you have some ideas on paper, start putting them into action! Your values are points of connection that will resonate with your ideal clients, so consider if you want to plan regular posts on social media, embed a charitable donation into your business model, support other entrepreneurs who are among underserved and underrepresented populations, or post a photo from the protest you went to over the weekend. The point isn't just to make a page of your values. The point is to put your values into every facet of what you do and how you do it.

Here are a few ideas of ways you can incorporate values into your business practices.
- Host webinars or workshops that reflect your core values.
- You don't have to do a workshop ON your values. But your values should inform how you conduct your workshop, such as delivering genuinely helpful information rather than using your workshop or webinar as a thinly veiled sales pitch (a distressingly common trend). Occasionally, I will put a specific value front and center with a workshop, like "How to Write Pain Points Without Punching the Bruise" or "The Witchy Feminist Way to Write Your About Page and Beat Impostor Syndrome."
- Offer sliding-scale pricing, or scholarships, or services at lower price ranges for clients with fewer resources. Community creator and author Carmen Spagnola has offered a sliding scale for her Numinous Network for years, allowing members to choose to pay $45, $60, or $75/month. A sliding scale and scholarships can also

work when you have prospects answer questions about their income and other relevant details, which slots them into a specific price tier. I prefer offering different levels of service at different price points.
- Partner with charities or organizations aligned with your values. You might slightly increase your rates so you can afford to donate to charity, with "5% of each sale goes to [charity]" featured on your website. If you offer a widely desirable service, you could put together a donation gift card to be raffled off at a charity event, which can be excellent advertising. Aligning your business with a cause not only brings in clients who value social responsibility, it can increase brand visibility. I donate my time and writing expertise to writing dog and cat bios for my local animal rescue, which I don't talk about or promote, but maybe I should.

Note: Please don't confuse being open about your values with *performing* them for marketing purposes. The first is authentic, while the second is easy to spot and entirely gross.

Reasonable concerns regarding values

Let's talk about the resistance, anxiety, overwhelm, and even dread that can come up when many people think of stating their values publicly. Hey, I get it. I blithely let my father assume I was a Republican for the longest time because I didn't want to get into it with him (it's not like I was going to change his mind—the man had Hilary Clinton toilet paper). Avoiding conflict is a natural human response, and if you've experienced trauma or lived in a house that didn't always feel safe, taking a stand where other people will judge you is terrifying.

Don't feel obligated to post your values, even as an ethical, heart-centric business owner. There is no law, no rule, and no kind person who will demand that of you if it causes you distress.

I do ask that you know what your values are, what you stand for, and what ideals you're willing to support or defend. They can guide you and your business behind the scenes.

But if you are harboring a rebellious heart and you just need a nudge to give it a voice, I offer you this:

You may get blowback, you may attract trolls, you may hurt someone's feelings if your choices differ from theirs, and you may get an annoyed phone call from your MAGA hat-wearing father. It's okay. Because you will also be lifted on the shoulders of people who share your values and find peace and relief in your presence. You will be surrounded by support, some tearfully saying "thank you, I needed to hear that" in your DMs. The benefits far outweigh the costs.

Some values-related resistance I've experienced is feeling overwhelmed by all the things I'd like to do, or feel like I should do, to take action on my values. Especially when there are people on the internet ready to criticize you for staying silent on current events. When you're feeling overwhelmed, remember: You don't have to support every cause, go to every protest (or any), or create socially conscious social media posts for every crisis. Some of my favorite ethical business coaches do not post anything political and don't react to current events on their social media, but they incorporate their values into every piece of content and offer they create.

And me? Crowds make me anxious so you're unlikely to find me at a protest, but in November 2024, just after the election, I offered a "Dismantle the Patriarchy Special," promising a free Loom Review of any page of copy for businesses empowering women. It was exhilarating and exhausting to get so many replies—I loved it. This offer aligned with my value of radical generosity, was timely (I wasn't the only one enraged by election results), and boosted my social media follower count and newsletter list, while delighting me with responses. Plus, while it wasn't the purpose of the free offer, many of the business owners who emailed me have since become repeat clients. I shared my values, took action, and met many new, delightful clients in the process.

In short: Do what you feel is important. Do it your own way. Be creative. And find ways to share your values that bring you joy.

Takeaways

1. **Add a values page to your website:** Stating your values creates connection with your people and helps your ideal clients feel comfortable and safe working with you. When adding a values page to your website, choose three (more than that can be overwhelming for your readers) and discuss why those values matter to you and how you bake them into how you run your business.
2. **Walk the talk:** Don't add a values page if you're not willing and able to live those values and infuse them into how you do business. That said, be creative in how you take action. It doesn't have to look the same as how other people are taking action. It has to work for you to be sustainable.
3. **Be the change you want to see:** A good way to start is to identify what changes you'd like to see in the broader business world. When you run your business the way you wish all businesses were run, you're blazing a trail for future business owners.
4. **Know your limits:** Define what you would never compromise on and use those boundaries to direct who you work with, how you work, and what you work on. This helps you identify wrong-fit clients who aren't likely to benefit from working with you because they hold different core values.
5. **Use your values to connect and filter:** Your values are an incredibly strong connection point between you and your audience, and you can use them as filters to draw in right-fit clients and repel the rest. Discuss your values openly in your content, highlight them on your website, and show how you're taking action on them.

CHAPTER 3

Getting Clear on Your VALUE

Not to be confused with *values* (see previous chapter). Your VALUE is what your ideal clients will gain by working with you. This is where most entrepreneurs freeze because they don't have the answer.

What value do your ideal clients get from working with you?

It's likely you don't have the answer either.

And if you *think* you have the answer, you might be mistaken because…

The only people who can answer what value you offer are: your ideal clients.

They will tell you what they need from you, they will tell you if they're getting it, and they will tell you if they're getting it in the way they *need* to succeed. If you don't have that information from them, you run the risk of trying to sell them something they don't need. Ever heard the phrase "He could sell ice to an Eskimo[9]"? Don't be that person.

First step: You need to know how to ask your ideal clients the right questions so they can give you helpful answers. HELLO, CUSTOMER RESEARCH!

---

[9] Note: Don't use the colonialist word "Eskimo;" the Inuit Circumpolar Council prefers the term "Inuit."

Here's the quick 'n dirty on how to establish offer-market fit and know the real value you deliver.

STEP 1: FORM AN "IDEAL-CLIENT HYPOTHESIS."

This is your best guess as to who needs your help, why they need it, and what they sincerely want to be able to do. What service are you offering or thinking of offering? What problem does it solve, what pain does it alleviate, what struggle does it make easier? What do you think these people will be able to do or do better after working with you?

NOTE: You are not niching by demographic here. You are not doing a "client avatar" exercise that says, "Sally is a 43-year-old overachiever from Minneapolis with three kids, an average annual household income of $180,000, and a master's degree in business administration." That will not help you as much as niching around a struggle, problem, or desire.

STEP 2: GO OUT AND FIND THE PEOPLE WHO HAVE THE PROBLEM YOU SOLVE.

If you don't solve a "problem," then find someone who needs what you've got. If you run into trouble with this step, return to Step 1 because it's time to reconsider.

Places to find people to interview who match your ideal-client hypothesis:

- Your extended network (colleagues, coworkers, family members, or friends may know people who need your help, and they may be willing to make an introduction *for research only*)
- Private Facebook groups (ask permission from the admins)
- Comment sections on Instagram posts

- Reddit, Quora, or other question/answer-oriented social platforms
- Local businesses who serve like-minded customers and who'll allow you to put flyers on their cork boards (coffee shops, Pilates and yoga studios, crystal shops, bookstores, etc.)

STEP 3: ASK FOR A CONVERSATION ONLY AND OFFER SOMETHING IN RETURN.

Invite the person you've identified as falling into your "ideal-client parameters" (i.e., they have the problem you help with and you wouldn't mind working with them for real) to have a 30-minute conversation with you. Keep the invite simple, clear, and friendly, like:

"Hi, I saw you talking about [their struggle/frustration] on [place] and I'm currently building a [service/product/offer] to help with that problem. I'm in the early stages of development and I would love to interview you to get more details, if you're open to it. The interview takes 20-30 minutes max and is for research only."

This is where ethics come back into play because if you were an *unethical* business owner, you could try to flip these conversations into sales calls by pushing for a sale. That creates an uncomfortable situation if they're expecting a research call, and if prospective interviewees feel like this could turn into a sales call, they'll be on the defensive and you won't get helpful answers. Also, it's rude. Sometimes, an interviewee will express interest in working with you on the research call, and if that happens, set up a separate call to discuss it.

If finding interview volunteers is a struggle, *bribe them*. Bribery in this context is more about showing appreciation for their time and giving them a small incentive to talk to you. This could be as simple as a gift card for coffee. I've *tried* not to use Starbucks for this because I'd rather support smaller businesses, but Starbucks works well *because* it's a huge chain—just go with it. I've tried sending tea, ceramics, and even local-to-the-recipient art, and it's far more complicated and time consuming than anyone needs. Keep it simple. Very few people will turn down a free latte. Another good thank-you gift is a free coaching call, or session in your modality, scheduled separately and focused solely on them.

Here are a few questions I like to include in these calls that help specifically with copy:

1. **Struggles and symptoms:** Can you tell me what you're currently struggling with? What is the hard part you haven't quite been able to fix, solve, manage, or improve on your own?
2. **Ideal outcomes:** What would you love to be able to do once you've solved this issue? What would your life be like? What kind of person would you be on the other side? How would you feel once you've achieved your goal? What would you *not* feel anymore once you've achieved your goal?
3. **What they've tried:** What have you tried to fix/solve/manage/improve this issue? (Ask for specific books, names of podcasts, modalities, etc.)
4. **What almost worked (or didn't):** Which of those worked part of the way and which didn't work?
5. **Support:** What kind of support would you need to finally succeed with this?

And don't forget to ask for their consent to use their exact words and phrases in your marketing copy! You don't need to attach their names to it (anonymity is fine; these aren't testimonials), but you will be using their language verbatim on your website, sales pages, emails, and ads.

After you've collected your answers, the next step is to categorize them. I make a document containing all of the answers and use a color code to highlight repeated themes or words. Often, these repetitions signal emotional pain points, unmet needs, or desires. When we get to the sales page in Chapter 5, you can use these to craft the all-important empathy section.

I'm also specifically looking for success gaps between what interviewees have tried and what they still need. When I write my sales page, I will translate these into specific promises, often using snippets of their exact words.

Of course, that means I also bake these promises into the offer itself.

Building better offers

When discussing how to structure offers with my clients, I've seen a tendency to copycat other businesses' offers. Sometimes it's because my client took a course or a program and they were specifically taught to sell a "high-ticket six-month program" or told to have a "tripwire offer" (this is a manipulative tactic designed to get the consumer to say yes to a small, inexpensive offer so they will be more likely to say yes to a more expensive one later). But when we went over their sales pages, I asked these clients: "Why did you structure your offer this way? Why is six months necessary for your people to succeed? Is this cheaper tripwire offer enough for them to see any results?" And I was met with blank stares. They hadn't thought about what their clients actually need to succeed; they only thought about what they might be able to sell. Not because they're bad or greedy people—but because nobody asked them these questions before.

I would encourage you to use the answers from your client research to create innovative offers that help your clients succeed where other, more cookie-cutter services, programs, and courses have failed. Then, you can write about why your offer is structured for success, how it's different from other options, and why it's more effective. You'll get the sales *and* strengthen your unique point of view.

As you conceptualize your offer, ask yourself:
1. What kind of experience does your client need to have their best chance at success? High touch (lots of time with you?) Low touch (DIY with minimal support?).
2. How long do most people need to do this work to see results? For example, most people will not see "abs in two weeks." What is a reasonable timeline for success?
3. If the experience and time they need to succeed is high touch and a long time, you'll likely price your offer accordingly high. Is there a way you can break it up into smaller successes along the way that might be more affordable? Note: You don't have to lock anyone into a long program—I worked with my business coach for years on a month-to-month basis because I saw how much my business benefited.

When building an offer based on client feedback and research interviews, it's tempting to ask them: "What would the perfect program/offer be for you?" In the apocryphal words of Henry Ford, "If I had asked people what they wanted, they would have said faster horses." It's not their job to create your offer for you—if they knew what they needed, they would have solved their problems already! Your job is to synthesize the information you receive about their problems, what they've tried, why their attempts haven't worked, and what they need instead—and create a truly innovative offer from that raw material.

There are many different types of value

I'm an action girl. I think in terms of "what can I do?!" But there are other types of value to consider when you're thinking of how you help people. For example, one of the things my clients say they love about working with me is "feeling so seen." I had no idea that was valuable (*what can you do with it?*), but it's been the cause of countless referrals. Your definition of value, or mine, is likely limited by what you perceive as valuable, but everyone has their own list. Here are a few types of value to consider:

1. Transformational value: How will your clients feel or what will their lives look like after working with you?
2. Monetary value: Does working with you save them money, make them money, or help them manage their money more confidently?
3. Convenience value: Do you make their lives or jobs easier or less stressful?
4. Social value: Will working with you help them gain respect, recognition, or a sense of belonging? Can you introduce them to individuals or groups who can help them reach their goals or find camaraderie? Do you make them feel seen, heard, and valued? Sometimes, the social value is spending time with you.
5. Emotional value: Feeling supported and cared for human to human is immeasurably valuable, and that's something solo service providers are able to provide better than larger companies. It's an advantage. Use it.

Takeaways

1. **Your value is about results:** Focus on how your ideal clients benefit from working with you, what they'll be able to do, and how they will feel. Form your offer structure to give them the best chance at success, rather than structuring your offer around what you think will sell better.
2. **Your clients define your value, not you:** Don't assume you know what your clients need and how they need your support to get it. Ask them! While it's tempting to skip customer research (because it's hard to find people to interview and talking to strangers is scary), it's a critical step to building a sustainable business.
3. **Don't let your interviewees tell you what to make:** You need to be a few steps ahead of your ideal clients and think of solutions they haven't. To do that, identify their core need (rather than their suggested solution) and brainstorm better ways to meet it. Everything they've tried that didn't work is a clue to what finally will work. For copy and offer purposes, ask what their struggle feels like, when it pops up in their day, and what they've already tried to fix it. When you write your copy, you'll use these answers to write an intro that is cinematically visual thanks to the specific details you gather.

CHAPTER 4

Charm, Pain, and the Lizard Brain

The most common manipulative tactics in copywriting and how to do the opposite

You know what bugs me? Self-help, leadership, and personal development books that have ONE good idea that could fit neatly into a blog post but bloat to 300 pages of "stories" that rehash the one good idea ad nauseam. It's a pet peeve that I vow never to repeat (and explains why this book is so short).

I want you to cultivate your pet peeves, too.

When I ask my students and clients what drives them crazy about writing for their businesses, the most frequent offender is:

Long, repetitive sales pages that go on forever and force you to scroll for ten minutes to find the price

What would you add to your pet peeves list? As you scroll through social media, your inbox, and other websites this week, keep a list of sales, marketing, and design tactics that rub you the wrong way. Start by identifying when something feels off, then try writing down what, exactly, bothers you. The more practice you get identifying and analyzing manipulative tactics, the better you can protect yourself as a consumer, and the better you will become at consciously choosing ethical alternatives in your own marketing.

My method is to keep a file in Google Docs for copywriting I like…and another file for social media posts, sales emails, and sales pages that burn my biscuits.

The ones that *burn my biscuits* are the ones I come back to again and again. They inspire me to consider how that marketing piece should have been done differently. And how I can flip it upside-down and do it better.

What I love about cultivating my pet peeves—recording them, keeping a list, visiting them for inspiration—is that by consciously doing the opposite with my own marketing, I have to get creative. I force myself to differentiate as a business owner and service provider in ways I never would have if I had only kept a file of marketing that I admire. (I'd be so tempted to copy those great posts rather than do something radically different.)

Here are five tactics that are easy to spot and blatantly manipulative to get you started on your pet-peeve foraging adventure.

Five common manipulative tactics (and flips)

1. LONG-FORM SALES PAGES (THAT ARE WAY TOO LONG)

Long-form sales pages aren't inherently problematic. The idea behind a long sales page is that when you have an offer that requires a significant commitment of time and/or money, your clients need more information to feel comfortable taking the risk. The page length should be proportional to how much information your clients need to feel confident about their investment.

The sinister side is when the sheer length is used to wear the reader down to an exhausted, malleable nub, much like when a car salesperson talks for three hours when you knew the car you wanted and the price you'd like to pay when you walked onto the lot. Many people will be worn down to the point of making poor decisions.

How do you know if a sales page is long because it needs to be or if it is using length to wear you down?

- It repeats itself. If it keeps going for pages AND repeats its points, it's trying to wear you down.
- It doesn't give you the necessary information to make the best decision for you. This may mean withholding the price until the sales call (i.e., there's a "book a call" button where you expect to find the price) or putting the price waaay down at the bottom of the page in small font so you have to wade through all of the sales copy to find it.
- It tells you nothing new or fresh about your problem, the offer provider's philosophy, or the solution. Instead, the page repeats pain points, paints a picture of how those symptoms could get even worse, and then paints more pictures of how your life will be perfect once you plonk down hard currency for their solution. (This is the Pain - Agitate - Solution formula, which we'll get to in Chapter 5.)

The Flip: Put the important details at, or near, the top of the page instead of at the bottom. Or at least make them easy to find if someone is scrolling to the bottom for them. Price point and time available MATTER as forms of fit and a prospect's available time and money aren't yours to negotiate.

Here are the "Need 2 Knows" I created for the sales page of my five-week copywriting program:

In this "Need 2 Knows" section, I use my favorite formula for clarity (which I also use in taglines) to describe the value of the offer: what it is, who it's for, and what it helps them do.

NEED 2 KNOWS

What's Happening Write the Home, About Services & Sales pages in 4 weeks with a pro holding your hand every step of the way in this small, group program

How Much $1000 (or 2 payments of $500)

Dates September 5th to October 7th (4 weeks of instruction, 1 additional week for revisions & questions)

Why It's different Learn ethical copywriting, use templates designed for coaches & service-based entrepreneurs, and have all of your work polished by me

12 spots available – so you get lots of personal attention

Then, I add an explanation about why this offer is different from what they've tried. I also include the dates, price, and spaces available.

You may think, "Oh no, if I just put my price at the top of the page, my readers will only see that and decide they can't afford it!"

Maybe. But if they can't afford it, do you want them to buy it? There's a popular idea among business coaches that business owners shouldn't worry about what prospective clients can or can't afford. After all, if they "really want it," they'll find a way to pay for it, right?

Listen, I don't want anyone going into debt so they can buy my program. I do worry about them. And I don't want my program to be an impulse or coerced purchase they'll regret later. Looking out for your prospects' best interests is not only the ethical choice—it also helps ensure the people who buy are able to commit without stress (and end up being much easier to work with!). So I try to make my offers as accessible as possible by offering payment plans. I also don't raise the price of extended payment plans.

2. NOT-SO-FREE "FREEBIES" (AKA NON-CONSENSUAL AND COERCIVE LIST-BUILDING)

This is one that almost everyone does or has done (including me because you don't know until you know). That "freebie" or "lead magnet" you use to build your email list? It's problematic.

First, if you call it a "freebie" but require people to give you their contact information to get it, it's not free. (Can we stop calling it a "freebie" please?)

Second, if you don't make it clear that when they give you their contact information they will automatically be put on your email list, that's non-consensual list-building. Email lists are like sex: You want enthusiastic consent that is clear, continuous, coercion-free, and conscious.

Third, even if you ARE transparent about adding folks to your list but all they really want is the lead magnet and feel like they have to "hand over" their email address to get it… that's coercion.

The Flip: You can still use lead magnets to build relationships but offer them up freely. As in: un-gated, for the taking, no contact info required. Then, in the actually-free freebie, invite them to join your email list (so they get even more value!) and follow you on social media. Give them buttons. Make it easy. Just don't make it a requirement.

Why it works: The whole point of your freebie is to offer a taste of what it's like to work with you. It should offer real value, tangibly help your prospective clients, and introduce why your approach is different (and more effective) than what they've already tried. Use it to build trust. Once your readers experience tangible value, they'll naturally want more and opt in to your list. And they'll do so enthusiastically. We will dive into all of this in Chapter 7.

3. URGENCY, SCARCITY, AND FOMO

FOMO (fear of missing out) is a psychological process wrapped up in scarcity and urgency that causes anxiety and fear of loss. The brain literally perceives danger when you *might not get something you might want* and puts you on high alert, making you more likely to take action to relieve the discomfort. Specifically, to take action *faster*, bypassing your logical thought processes.

The lizard brain (the primal part of the brain that hasn't evolved since humans stopped walking on their knuckles[10]) knows that resources are limited. To survive, you need resources. The other option is death.

The lizard brain does not understand that countdown timers for programs are not life-or-death scenarios. It thinks,

---

10 The term "lizard brain" refers to a concept, popularized by Paul MacLean in the 1960s, that describes a primitive part of the human brain called the "reptilian complex," which is thought to be responsible for basic survival instincts like fight-or-flight responses. Modern neuroscience says it's a myth, but modern marketers are still very into it.

"Oh crap, there is a limited resource. I might need it. I might want it! I'd better act now or it will go away!"

This panic bypasses the more evolved parts of the brain that would, given time, ask, "Do I really need this? Would that money be better spent elsewhere?"

Mainstream marketers treat the logical mind as the enemy to be bypassed, tricked, worn down into submission, or as "objections" to be "coached" around.

Ethical copywriters, however, want to help the logical mind stay in control by not triggering fear through false or unnecessary urgency, scarcity, or FOMO.

You'll see these three tactics at play in:
- Countdown timers: The goal is to speed up the decision by hammering the point home that this opportunity will disappear in 3, 2, 1 seconds.
- "Cart closes in…" emails: Sometimes these are true. If the cart closes tomorrow, by all means, say so. That is true urgency. But I've seen "Cart closes in…" emails followed up with days of emails extending the deadline while offering more deals and incentives. The cart didn't actually close. That is false urgency.
- "Only one spot left!" emails: Sometimes you do have limited seating, and if there are just a few spots (or one) left, you should tell people. But I've seen "just one spot left!" emails go out when there A) was not a cap on participation or B) the offer was only half-filled at best.

Here's the sticky wicket: Countdown timers are manipulative. They trigger anxiety and are explicitly designed to hasten action. You can tell people a date without triggering anxiety. I've yet to hear an argument that persuades me to use countdown timers.

True urgency is okay to use. Your cart closes on a certain day. Your program starts on a certain day. You should communicate those facts. Do the same with the actual number of spots you have available if they're limited.

I like to take the anxiety out as much as possible, even when something is true, because I want my readers to think about it before they commit to an investment. So, instead of speeding up the sale, I ask myself, "How can I slow this sale down so they have time to think?"

The Flips
- Instead of a countdown timer, just give the actual dates and stick to them.
- If the offer (course, program, workshop) is available in the future, say so. And if you don't know when you'll be offering it again, say so. If you know for a fact you will never be offering it again, say so. Real scarcity isn't unethical to use.
- You don't need to tell the world that you've only half-filled your program and are desperate to fill the remaining seats (I love transparency, but desperation is off-putting). Mention "Only three spaces left" when it's true. Before that point, you can offer creative and helpful incentives. One I like to use is, "The earlier you buy, the longer the payment plan." This helps people on smaller budgets *and* incentivizes them to commit if they're ready.

These aren't just gray areas—they're spectrums of gray. For example, I've read arguments that countdown timers *help* folks with ADHD because the urgency facilitates focus and timely decision-making. (I don't buy this argument, but I've heard it!) Do what feels right to you, but be aware that when you're trying to influence someone to take action on *your* timeline, triggering fear is often involved.

I prefer to create space for logic.

4. PRICE FRAMING

You've probably seen this section on sales pages before—it's very common. It's the "what you get" part that explains everything you will receive after clicking the "buy now" button. Often, it also includes "bonuses." Giving details about what people will get is great, but once you add price framing, you've sunk your credibility. Here's what price framing looks like in practice.

In The Ultimate Leadership Ascension Accelerator™ online, self-paced course, you will get:
- Access to the Membership Portal (The Vault of Vibes™): Five self-paced modules that unlock the sacred Lead with Impact Formula™—the one true path to unleashing your inner CEO goddess archetype. Templates? Check. PDFs? Naturally. Guided by PowerPoint? You bet. (a $6,000 value)
- Access to a private Facebook community to help you stay on track and inspired with other high-achieving professionals just like you! (a $97 value)

- One private 120-minute VIP coaching call personalized to your career goals. This is a personalized deep dive where we whisper affirmations to your LinkedIn profile and manifest you a corner office and a snack drawer. **(a $1,000 value)**
- Mini-Course Bundle: The Leadership Ladder™ Expansion Pack: Because what's better than one course? Five bonus ones that you'll totally finish, probably. **(a $1,500 value)**
  - Five Steps to Lead with Love: quick start guide to light a fire under your team
  - Negotiate with Confidence: set reasonable productivity goals for your team and ask for a raise at the same time (and get it)
  - LinkedIn for Thought Leaders—make your reputation and build your legacy
  - The Art of the Steal: Taking the cream-of-the-crop talent from other departments to make your team even better
  - Life Purpose Statement Generator™ because your leadership presence in the office is only as strong as your leadership presence in life
- LIVE virtual office hours bi-monthly for three months: your questions answered by my team of highly trained chihuahuas! **(a $3,000 value)**

Total Program Value: $11,597
Special Offer: $2,997!

If you are ending any line item with "a $XXXX value!"—and you are not actually selling that additional item/product/

recording elsewhere on your website for that price—where are you pulling that number from? Thin air? Maybe not. Maybe you have a reason for slapping that price tag onto something that should just be baked into your offer because it's what your clients need to succeed with you. But if you are not selling it a la carte, do not list it as a separate and additional "value."

Why? It reads as lying. Most of the time, it is lying. It's picking a big number out of the clear blue sky to inflate the perceived value of your offer so prospects feel like they're getting a better deal than they truly are.

That is price framing in a nutshell: inflating the perceived value of your offer by sectioning off each part with a fake "a la carte" price, then giving your "package price" that is much, much lower than the combined total.

There is no gray area here. This is inherently manipulative and designed to trick the readers into thinking they're getting a deal.

I know good business owners with great programs who use this tactic, so I'm not judging the person. But I am asking you to question where you get your numbers. Are they true, and (even if they are true) could they leave readers with the impression that you're lying?

Because this tactic really does undermine credibility.

However, I have seen price framing used in a completely ethical way that made readers aware of the superlative value they were really getting. Tad Hargrave, founder of Marketing for Hippies, used this technique on a sales page—and it was effective because he included ebooks and mini-courses that he actually sold, "a la carte," for those prices elsewhere on his website. They were truly bonuses that people were glad to get and could verify the value for themselves.

Yes, you can use bonuses if:
- They are, in fact, bonuses, and not workbooks, videos, or resources that are necessary to succeed in the program. If they're necessary, then they should be baked into the main program, not offered as "extras."
- You sell them elsewhere on your website. In which case, lose the "valued at" language and instead say "priced at" or "I sell these for $XX a la carte."

You may also want to use a bonus as an incentive for early signups, which does create some urgency, but I don't see it doing harm. Your call.

The Flips
- Don't put (Valued at $XXX) with your itemized list of what they get—unless you're actively selling that individual product elsewhere for that price.
- Give the total price of the offer, and/or the payment plan breakdown. If there's an early-bird discount, you can include that, too. Just don't artificially inflate the price only to slash it in half like a 1990s late-night infomercial.

5. CHARM PRICING

Closely related to price framing is charm pricing: ending your price number with .99, .97, or .95 instead of a round number. For example, $9.99 instead of $10.

Charm pricing is a purely psychological manipulative tactic that relies on how the brain reads numbers. People in Western cultures read left to right, with judgments of numerical differences anchored on the leftmost digit. Simply put, the number you see first is the one that sticks in your mind. Charm prices use the left-digit effect to make a product appear cheaper than it is, bypassing the conscious choice of the buyer.

It's a simple choice for business owners: $297 is manipulative while $300 is not. And don't tell me you use $999 because it's your angel number. I believe angels are solidly on the side of ethical marketing, too.

These tactics survive because they're everywhere. "Everyone" uses them. And when you see things done one way everywhere, it's natural to accept that's just how they're done.

But when you start choosing to do things differently, you show everyone else there are options! Suddenly, "everyone" isn't using these practices. Eventually, these practices can become unacceptable.

The Flips
- Use whole numbers—no .99 nonsense.
- If you're closer to the higher number, round up.

Neurolinguistic programming in copywriting

I can't discuss manipulative marketing practices without mentioning neurolinguistic programming (NLP). It's a hot topic in copywriting, marketing, and sales circles. Even though NLP began as a legit therapy tool, cults, MLMs, and pickup artists are notorious for using it. As my mother says, "You're judged by the company you keep."[11]

The terminology used in NLP is deliberately obtuse (academic

---

[11] Aesop originated this as "a man is known by the company he keeps," circa the sixth century B.C.E. It's an oldie but goodie.

language that sounds impressive but tells you little) and makes you feel like you need years of study to understand it. My area of expertise is translating jargon into plain language, and I'm here to tell you: It's smoke and mirrors. Here's what you need to know:

NLP, as it is used in marketing, is a set of observations of how the human brain takes in information and makes emotional connections that can lead to liking, trusting, and building unfounded hopes—which leads to taking action.

It's not magic or mind control (the people who say it is are invested in you buying an NLP course from them). Just a dash of critical thinking bursts the NLP bubble.

That said, you'll hear a lot of people talking about it, so let's talk about it, too, because it is a technique used by people trying to be manipulative.

Here's where NLP techniques show up in copywriting (these are just writing techniques, so don't get hung up on the term "NLP").

1. STORYTELLING

I love telling a good story to connect with my readers on a human-to-human level. Humans evolved with storytelling: It's baked into our DNA. Using storytelling to make an emotional connection (as you do with sales pages and about pages) is an NLP technique because human brains are wired to respond to stories by *neural coupling* (seeing yourself in the characters in stories), *mirroring* (feeling the emotions you read about), and releasing dopamine to help remember the story.

For these reasons, stories are effective at establishing emotional connection. That's what the first "empathy" section of a sales page does: It holds up a mirror to your readers' experiences so they see themselves reflected (NLP "mirroring").

You'll read more about how to do that in Chapter 5.

Storytelling isn't inherently bad or manipulative here because you're using it as an ethical business owner to establish fit. People who don't see themselves in this story are not your ideal clients.

In fact, much of NLP copywriting is just basic communication, but other NLP-informed copywriting practices are more problematic.

2. FUTURE PACING

The "imagine if" section, found in far too many sales pages, is one of the worst offenders; it's a technique called "future pacing."

"Imagine if," "what would it be like if," "visualize this," "what if you could," "envision a world where" all demand that readers picture a scenario of flawless, idealized success—which the program or offer isn't actually promising and in no way guarantees. It's just asking you to "imagine" what it would be like if everything went perfectly. This tricks your brain into believing that the program/offer/course you're buying can and will deliver those results when there is no way that promise can be made.

For example, in a sales video for a program on creating courses, the host says:

*"Imagine if you launched that course throughout the year and it got better and better. You make $100,000 *snap* just like that."*[12]

While future pacing in marketing often sets readers up with unrealistic expectations, it's incredibly helpful within the therapeutic context it was intended for. The benefits of visualization are well documented. Multiple studies show that athletes

---

[12] Direct quote from the Digital Course Academy sales video, minute seven, with Amy Porterfield and Laura Belgray.

who practice visualization techniques experience significant improvements in accuracy, speed, and consistency. Sadly, this does not translate to making $100,000 *snap* just like that.

3. POWER WORDS

Mostly, NLP gets into ethical copy problems by trying to use "power words" (emotionally evocative words) to subconsciously compel readers to feel a certain way. Using words like "imagine" is the subconscious equivalent of telling someone "Don't think about a pink rhinoceros." Of course, they're going to think about the pink rhinoceros. But other words, like "secrets," "exclusive," "effortless," "instantly," or "proven" (by whom? when? show me the study!) are there to make you:

1. Feel like you're getting something other people can't get (they can)
2. Believe it's going to require no effort (never true)
3. Assume it's guaranteed to work (unless they're offering your money *and time* back, it isn't)

The ethical choice is simple: Don't lie in your copy. The hard part is recognizing when the words you're using—words that everybody uses—can't be substantiated and should probably be left out.

If you'd like to check your existing copy for manipulative tactics, here's a quick checklist:
- Clarity: Does this page make information easily accessible?
- Consent: Is the reader making a fully informed choice that hasn't been artificially "sped up?"
- Care: Does this copy prioritize the reader's best interests?

Takeaways

1. **Cultivate your pet peeves:** Identify and document manipulative tactics that annoy you in marketing. Use these as inspiration to do the opposite, fostering creativity and differentiation in your approach.
2. **Don't just write long sales pages because you think you're supposed to:** Write what your ideal clients need to know and stop there. Let them decide. (I'll show you how to do that in the next chapter.)
3. **Align with logic, not fear:** Ethical marketing supports logical decision-making rather than bypassing it with tactics designed to exploit anxiety or FOMO. Slow down the sale to encourage thoughtful choices.
4. **If it feels icky, question it:**
    - Is it trying to fool//fake/manipulate?
    - Does it have to be that way?
    - Can you do the opposite? What could that look like?
    - How can you empower the consumer to make the best decision *for them*?
5. **Respect the reader's autonomy:** Avoid tactics like overly long sales pages, coercive "freebies," false urgency, and price framing. These strategies undermine trust by manipulating readers into decisions they might later regret.
6. **Clarify and simplify:** Provide crucial details like pricing, dates, and availability up front to empower your audience to make informed decisions without pressure or hidden obstacles.
7. Reconsider NLP techniques: While storytelling can

establish fit, techniques like future pacing ("imagine if...") and overusing power words often mislead by triggering unrealistic expectations.

CHAPTER 5

How to Write a Non-Icky Sales Page

The sales page (aka landing page) is the most potentially problematic page you will write for your business, and it's the one heart-centered business owners struggle to write the most. Why?
Because:

A. THE PRESSURE IS ON TO SELL.

This page is mainly responsible for keeping little Brady in braces (or, if you're me, keeping your mini schnauzer's cookie jar filled with fancy dog treats). But it's not just your ability to pay bills at stake. It's also your perception of yourself as a capable business owner. You have ego, money anxiety, and desire pushing you to try your best to make a sale.

B. PRESSURE LEADS TO PANIC.

When you feel desperate to make money, you're more likely to try methods that other people tell you made *them* money, even if those tactics make you feel the ick. Some values-driven business owners who refuse to compromise slide into not marketing at all because they don't know of non-icky options that work. Which means nobody knows about your business and the offer you worked so hard to build gets few (if any) takers. I've seen this happen far too many times with amazing coaches and phenomenal offers because they weren't willing to compromise their values (yay!) but didn't know of an effective alternative to spread the word (nooo!).

In this chapter, you will see where sales pages get the ick[13]—and how you can write them effectively, without feeling sleazy, to bring in right-fit clients who love you. Keep in mind where I draw the line is subject to my code of ethics and values. Yours may differ.

If *my* advice gives you the ick, I want you to think about why and how you can invent a better way to connect with your clients that feels good. Then, test it because our goal is marketing with ethics *and* efficacy.

Here is my approach to the sales page.

A SALES PAGE IS NOT:
- Where you convince someone to buy from you.
- Where you get readers hyped up and excited about the results they dream of getting but that you cannot realistically or honestly promise.
- Where you deliver all of your program or course material (over-educating won't serve you or your readers on this page).
- Where you need to withhold information that will genuinely help your readers have "aha" moments about their problems and gain insights into what makes your approach unique. This usually happens when there's a

---

13 My definition of "the ick" is the feeling that rises up in your stomach when you experience something gross or have to do something gross. Like forgetting your scalpel at the sixth grade science fair and having to dissect a sheep's eyeball with your fingernails minutes before the parents show up (which, yes, I did—and it made me a much more organized adult who makes lists of everything). That is the ick. You should not feel the ick when writing your copy or sharing your marketing.

fear of "giving away the secret recipe." Or the thought "if I tell people exactly what I'm doing, why would they buy it?" I don't believe you need to worry about either of those things, and if you withhold too much about how your process works, you erode trust with your audience.
- Where you "empower" your readers to take responsibility for all of their problems *without* acknowledging the underlying causes contributing to those problems. The factors that make your clients' struggles harder are often societal, cultural, familial, economical, and outside of any one person's control. Toxic positivity (aka "high vibes only!") and the "pull yourself up by the bootstraps" mentality—even beliefs in manifestation—can fall into the trap of making the victim feel wholly responsible, which means they feel guilt and shame rather than questioning these systems and feeling appropriate outrage.

A SALES PAGE SHOULD…
- Signal to your right-fit potential clients that they are in the right place.
- Make your ideal client feel seen and understood.
- Help readers determine if this is the answer they've been searching for if your approach is right for them and if your point-of-view resonates with theirs.
- Tell your readers something they haven't yet considered about their problem, its cause(s), and its solution.
- Give the consumer all the information they need to make the right decision *for them*.

When I wrote my sales page for my Truer Copy Mastermind—a five-week crash course to write your entire website with lots of personal support—I thought hard about what felt icky to me about sales pages.

I didn't like:
- The length (long for no reason other than to wear the reader down).
- Scrolling for the information I actually wanted (like the price).
- Needless repetition.
- Feeling like I was trapped in a corner by a used car seller who kept wanting to talk me into buying (okay, that's talking about length and repetition again, sorry).

So when I sat down to write, I centered myself with this mantra:

What do my readers need to know to make the best decision for them?

And with that, I wrote the outline of my sales page.

Sales Page Outline
1. Need 2 Knows
2. Header + clear tagline
3. Empathy intro (where they are now)
4. What they've tried
5. Why their problem is hard to solve
6. My POV origin story
7. The Way That Works
8. Offer details + CTA + testimonials
9. Fit check
10. Fear Soother Section (FAQs)

You will see slight variations of this structure in many copywriting courses. The sections will be called different things, but if you look at the job of each section—they're doing the same job. The ethical copywriting difference is how (and sometimes when) you do those jobs.

The essential jobs:
- Need 2 Knows are pure logistics and practical fit checks. (Do I have the time? Do I have the money?) Most traditional sales pages put this section at the bottom, or don't include it at all (moving the reader to a high-pressure sales call instead).
- Header + clear tagline that answer the questions: "Is this the solution for the problem I have?" "Is this offer what I need?"

- Empathy intro shows that you deeply, vividly understand your reader's experience, pain, or desires (sometimes all three).
- What they've tried tells your reader you know where they've been and it gives you a foundation for explaining why your approach is different (your point of view).
- Why their problem is hard to solve develops your point of view further because you're explaining where you believe their problems are coming from.
- My POV origin story is the autobiographical story of how you figured this out and found The Way That Works.
- The Way That Works is where you describe your unique solution.

And the rest of the page, really, is more logistics, some social proof, a fit check, and at least one big bright "buy" button.

What I find interesting about the above structure is how often I find myself switching sections around. I've discovered that, as long every section is on the page, it doesn't seem to matter what order they're in. You can put the Need 2 Knows at the bottom, throw them in the middle, stack them in a column on the side—doesn't matter. You could lead with your POV origin story, or The Way That Works and then work backward to how you figured it out. When I teach this page to my students, I often recommend that they write each section on a 3x5 card so they can play with the order that feels like the best flow for them.

Many copywriting programs and templates treat copywriting like building an engine: You need all the right parts and they have to be put in the right places for the sales machine to work. For me, it's more like making soup. Put the vegetables in first, and they'll get a little caramelization to build the flavor, but you're not going to ruin anything if you pour water in first and add your vegetables later. That said, please keep the header and tagline at the top (before or after the Need 2 Knows), or your soup will be extremely confusing.

Part 1: Need 2 Knows

As I've mentioned, I put my Need 2 Knows section at the top of the page instead of at the bottom (where others usually place it). One of my students calls this the "TL;DR section"[14] (love it!).

A Need 2 Knows, or logistics summary, section at the top acts as an aside to the audience, breaking the fourth wall[15] and speaking human to human instead of seller to consumer. And it FREAKS people OUT! Some readers told me they automatically scrolled to the bottom, looking for the price and dates, before they figured out those details were at the top!

This surprise strategy (because *it was strategic*) shook my readers out of their "ugh, I'm being sold to" autopilot mode. They paid closer attention to the rest of the page because, if I was doing something so radical and transparent at the beginning... *What on earth was I going to do next?!*

 *When you identify something that feels icky or is a pet peeve in marketing (like hiding the most important details) and consciously choose to do something else, it forces you to get creative and be original. It's a deer trail that shows you a way to differentiate yourself in a crowded market by doing what other business owners aren't. And it gets people's attention.*

---

14   TL;DR = "too long; didn't read"
15   Theater reference. The fourth wall is an imaginary barrier that separates the audience from the actors on stage or characters in a film. In this case, your audience is your readers.

That said, a lot of business owners are nervous about trying this on their own sales pages because they've been told that they need to "overcome objections" to make the sale. Believe me, you don't want someone in your program who doesn't have the time (so they're late to calls or never attend them) or are financially stressed because they've gone into debt to pay for your course (stressed people will create stress for you, often asking for more than you're prepared to deliver to "get their money's worth"). You're not just protecting them, you're protecting yourself.

What to include in your Need 2 Knows section:
1. What your clients or students will be doing with you, for how long, and a hint about why they want your solution (e.g., "a six-week course to learn SEO *without* crying over complicated tech").
2. How much it will cost and if there is a payment plan.
3. Dates and time commitment.
4. Why your offer is more effective than other things they've tried.
5. Availability, if spaces are limited.

Keep it short and to the point. Design-wise, I like to put this section in its own box or graphic with a slightly different background color so it pops.

As you can tell, I am firmly part of *Team Put the Price on the Sales Page*. And not just *on* the sales page but at the top of the sales page. But maybe you're wondering, "Well, why wouldn't you put the price on the sales page? People need to know, right?"

Here are some arguments I've heard from business owners and business coaches in favor of hiding the price:

- "My services are entirely bespoke. I can't quote a price until I know the client's needs."
    - This is part true and part BS.[16] I do a lot of custom packages for my clients and, on my sales page for custom copywriting support, I list static prices when possible, show a price range, or say "prices start at…" when I don't have an exact number. I have a "no bad surprises" policy, so I want to make sure everyone knows what to expect before we even schedule a call. Transparency leads to trust, and trust leads to sales, referrals, and more sales.

- "If I put my price on the sales page, people will only look at the price and not read further."
    - This is fair. Price is a crucial piece of fit criteria, and if your readers can't afford it, they don't need to read further. The cost has to fit into their budget. If your offer is a fit except for the price, and you are articulating the value well (especially in the header and tagline copy!), they may decide it's worth investigating further and might be worth the splurge. They may not. That's fine.

- "Your prospect doesn't know the real value of your offer; you have to demonstrate it on a sales call."
    - This may be true if your copy is unclear on your sales page, but then you have bigger problems.[17] You

---

16 That's *bullshit*.
17 Yes, even if you have a hard-to-explain modality that has to be seen/felt/experienced to be understood. You can still articulate the value on a sales page. I do this for my clients every day (*hello, somatic coaches*).

absolutely can and should articulate the value of your offer on your sales page, so when people book a call, they are already excited to work with you (and feel confident knowing exactly what to expect, including the price). The "value" can be the results your clients will get, what they will be able to do, or the intrinsic pleasure of the experience—it doesn't always have to be tangible. When you clearly articulate the value on the page, the call becomes a final fit check to ensure you both benefit from working together.

- "Most people have 'money mindset issues' and think they can't afford something when they actually can: You just need to coach them around the money objection."
  - If you don't put the price on the sales page, the prospect has to book a call where you can "coach them" around their "money mindset issues" and get them to buy from you. You're essentially saying, "Hey, your gut instinct (or reasonable knowledge of your budget) are beliefs that don't serve you!" This is gaslighting (e.g., "That thing you've observed? You didn't see that. It's all in your head.") and undermines people's trust in themselves. Do some people have money mindset issues? Absolutely. But all people have budgets that deserve our respect. Budgets are a healthy boundary. This is why I never try to "coach" someone out of a price objection or "help people say yes to themselves," as I've heard it called. Treat your clients like adults who are capable of making their own decisions.

Each of these arguments does the opposite of empowering the consumer to make the best decision for them. Fortunately, there's a growing backlash among consumers, and many refuse to work with anyone who doesn't put a price or price range on a sales page.

Part 2: Empathy intro

This is where you show how well you know your ideal client and what they're going through. It's the copy equivalent of offering a friend a tight hug after they've had a hard day. This section also acts as a filter, so your right-fit clients know you're speaking to them and wrong-fit clients think, "Oh, this isn't for me," and go away.

A central part of ethical business practices is to try to only accept right-fit clients who are likely to succeed with you *and* love the experience of working with you. Unethical business practices result from selling as much as possible to as many as possible as quickly as possible without worrying whether buyers get the support they need to achieve the results they paid for.

You only want right-fit clients—people who have the problem you help with and are likely able to succeed with the support you offer.

In the empathy intro, you lay out the problem by describing what your right-fit clients are experiencing right now—using storytelling to paint a picture of their lived experience and what their struggles are really like.

With this story, you're establishing problem-solution fit… *Do they have the problem or struggle you help with?*

Questions to ask yourself about your right-fit clients when you're writing the empathy intro:
- What are they feeling right now?
- What are they frustrated by?
- What do they want?
- What are they worried about?
- Where and when do these struggles peak? Exactly where—what location? Exactly when—time of day?

Think about this as describing the symptoms they're aware of that lead to your diagnosis of the cause.

Beware of the sinister potential of this section because what I call "empathy" others call "pain points." I'm not just switching words around—the approaches to an "empathy" section and a "pain point" section are very different.

PAIN POINTS VS. EMPATHY

The pain-pointy intro is a classic technique you'll see on almost every sales page (and in every drug company commercial) for a reason. It's part of the PAS copywriting formula:

Problem: Describe the reader's symptoms/where and how the problem shows up in their lives.

Agitate: Exaggerate the severity and urgency of the problems to heighten the reader's anxiety.

Solution: Reveal your solution and how it solves all of their problems.

The ethical issue is primarily with agitation because you're not only reflecting back to the reader the reality of how their problem shows up in their lives, but how much *worse* it could get. When you're a business owner (or a copywriter), not a psychic, this future-forecasting is nothing but emotional manipulation. Here's what agitation looks like if we break it down:

- Using vivid examples to show them how much worse it could get if they don't take action now. The examples are often slightly, or greatly, exagerrated from what might reasonably occur since the goal is to increase anxiety.
- Intentionally creating more discomfort and urgency (aka panic) to activate the lizard brain's survival instincts and bypass the logical mind.
- Presenting your solution as the only relief from the pressure you just created.

Here's what it might look like in practice—notice how subtle it can be:

Problem: Are you tired of watching everyone else succeed while you're stuck in the same place, working long hours for a paycheck that barely covers your bills? You see them flaunting their success on Instagram, talking about six-figure launches, and living lives of freedom while you can't even figure out where to start. Does it feel like no matter how hard you try you're just not cut out for this marketing game?

Agitate: Let's be honest: That sinking feeling of being left behind isn't just frustrating—it's humiliating. Every time you scroll through your feed, it's like a knife twisting deeper. You're not only missing out on the financial freedom you deserve; you're losing time—time that you'll never get back. What if you're stuck here forever, spinning your wheels, while everyone else speeds past you, building wealth and enjoying their dream lives? It's not just a lack of knowledge holding you back—it's costing you your future.

Solution: But here's the truth they don't tell you: Marketing isn't about working harder; it's about working smarter. And you don't need years of experience or a fancy degree to hit multiple six- and even seven-figure goals. My step-by-step program will take you from zero to marketing hero in just six weeks, giving you the exact blueprint to transform your income, your confidence, and your life—starting today.

The whole idea is to leverage fear, guilt, and shame so prospects buy into your solution quickly. I call this "punching the bruise."

The solution part of PAS is problematic, too, because many copywriting programs and business coaches recommend positioning your solution as the <u>only</u> solution.

You've found *one* way that works—and that is important. That is what sets your offer apart. It's the result of your lifetime of experience, training, education, practice, and body of work with the problem.

But as soon as you cross into "my way is the only way," you're heading into cult leader territory. That never ends well.

You don't want to position yourself as the only option or invalidate all the other options. Sure, if there's a common modality that you think is a dumpster fire, call it out (you're allowed to have opinions—just be prepared for the consequences). But I always give credit where it's due when other methods of achieving an outcome are concerned. If I take issue with a dominant modality or paradigm, I carefully explain why. This enriches my point of view and builds even stronger relationships with my ideal clients.

SHOULD WE JUST THROW PAIN OUT? NOT SO FAST

After seeing the potential for harm with the PAS formula, it's tempting to throw the whole thing out, vow never to use pain points in your copy, and subscribe entirely to the "High Vibes Love and Light" ideology.

I don't recommend going to that extreme. You run the risk of bypassing or ignoring your reader's very real pain, leaving them feeling unseen and potentially misunderstood.

When I teach empathy and pain points in my workshops, it's usually to an audience who comes in already sure that they do *not* want to use pain points. They've seen pain used to make people feel worse too many times and they do not want that kind of negativity in their copy. I like to tell this story to explain why I choose to acknowledge pain when it's present.

Picture yourself in a cafe, waiting to meet a friend. You sit down with a mug of hot tea and a pastry and wait. And wait. Your friend is late. Suddenly, she comes rushing in, saying, "Sorry, sorry, sorry! My cat threw up on the carpet just as I was leaving, I got a speeding ticket on the way, and I couldn't find parking, so I had to run three blocks to get here—I'm SO sorry!"

How would you greet your friend if she came in with this frazzled, frantic, stressed energy? You'd probably say something like, "Oh, honey, I'm so sorry, that's terrible! Have a seat, take a few deep breaths, I'm going to go order you a nice calming tea—want a cookie?"

You would acknowledge her pain before doing anything else. You would meet her where she is and then try to soothe her into feeling better. If you didn't acknowledge her emotional state and the difficulties she's been through, it wouldn't just be awkward…you'd sound like an insensitive jerk.

When I know my reader is coming to the page already in pain, already frustrated, feeling alone, anxious, maybe even desperate, I want to meet them exactly where they are and acknowledge what they're feeling and why those feelings are valid. But I don't leave them in the depths of despair, and I certainly don't make them feel worse about it to sell my solution.

Here's my formula for an empathy-filled intro that leaves manipulation behind:

Empathy: Talk about what's going on for your reader right now, addressing their struggle and what it looks like in their lives to show you understand it. Don't exaggerate.

POV: Reflect back to your reader what they've already tried, maybe what you've also tried, and why it didn't work or didn't work all the way.

A solution: Explain the solution you've found and why—in your experience—it is more effective. It's not the only way that works, but it just might work better for them.

You could call this formula EPA, but I believe the Environmental Protection Agency has already claimed that one.

Here's what this could look like in practice:

Empathy: It's exhausting to feel like you're spinning your wheels, trying to build something meaningful but not knowing how to get it in front of people. You've probably spent hours watching videos to get a handle on the basics, like how to create an Instagram strategy, or the difference between Reels, Stories, posts, and whatever the latest app offers. The tech is confusing, the advice on strategy is conflicting, and it's so overwhelming you're tempted to just hire someone. If only you had two grand a month burning a hole in your back pocket to pay a professional.

POV: I've been there, too. I tried piecing together free resources, following advice that sounded good but didn't actually help (or was outdated by a month, during which all the technology changed). I spent more time than I'd like to admit on strategies other people said worked for them but went nowhere for me. For so many solopreneurs, the problem isn't a lack of information—it's a lack of clear, practical guidance that fits their needs and experience level.

Solution: That's why I created [course name]. It's a straightforward, beginner-friendly program that cuts through the noise and focuses on what actually works, with technology explained at beginner levels and updated every time there's a change. You'll get a simple, actionable plan with video walkthroughs for marketing your business online, even if you've never done it before. It's not the only approach out there, but it's the one that's worked for me and for countless others who were feeling just as stuck as you are now.

This version focuses on understanding the reader's situation, sharing a relatable perspective, and offering a solution that feels approachable and grounded in experience. Here, I maintain focus on the problem and solution without stirring up emotions or using speculative language. It's clear, factual, and grounded in the ways my offer bridges the success gaps I've witnessed in other programs, courses, and approaches.

Emotions are compelling—that's how humans are wired! But appealing to the logic mind gains trust because you're not delivering hype. You're giving them reasonable, practical, hope.

Part 3: What they've tried

Your ideal clients have an issue, a struggle, a desire they haven't been able to attain, maybe even something painful they'd like to alleviate or heal—and you are likely not their first stop on the road to figuring it out. People are amazing that way. They'll usually try to find a solution before paying someone else good money to do it for them. So the easy-to-DIY problems don't tend to create profitable niches for business owners.

This means your prospective client has already tried to solve their problem, possibly in many ways. Your job is to list those ways so readers know you understand where they're coming from.

This is a short section. Really, just a bullet point list. The key is to make each bullet point specific.

You're not going to get that level of specificity by guessing (guessing is the easiest way to come up with answers that "look right," but if you build your business on guesswork, *my guess* is you won't be in business for long). The specificity will come from conversations you have with people who fit into your ideal client parameters.[18] Ask them what they've tried, who they've listened to, what they've read, and how well that went. Make sure to get the names of modalities they've used, experts and influencers they follow, and titles of podcasts they've listened to and books they've read.

Then your list goes from: "You've listened to podcasts" to "You've listened to the *Maintenance Phase* podcast" (I love that one). Not just "You've read books," but instead, "You've read books like *Crooked: Outwitting the Back Pain Industry and Getting on the Road to Recovery* by Cathryn Jakobson Ramin" (another personal favorite). Specificity is what makes copy work. The more specific you get, the more your readers will see themselves reflected in your words.

Even if they listen to *We Can Do Hard Things* instead of *Maintenance Phase* (it doesn't have to be the same to work).

What they've tried may include:
- Healing modalities, like yoga, Reiki, craniosacral therapy (list which ones, and the results they saw, or didn't see)
- Mainstream approaches like seeing a doctor or therapist (what happened? What were they told? Was it harmful,

---

18 See Chapter 3 for bribery with coffee.

helpful, or in between?)
- Spiritual approaches (which ones? What happened?)
- Listening to podcasts, reading books, watching videos (did they gain insight, or just more anxiety about their problem?)
- Crowdsourcing answers online or talking to friends (what kinds of advice did they read? What exactly did their friends tell them?)

When you show your prospects that you know where they are now *and* where they've been, you're proving that you GET them.

Then it's time to connect the dots between what they've tried, read, or listened to and how well those methods worked.

If they're talking to you now, their previous attempts to find solutions didn't work out as well as they'd hoped. You're going to reflect this in your copy with a line like "These solutions didn't entirely fix the issue because…" and launch into what you believe is the missing piece.

When you're gathering this data about what they've tried and why it didn't work, you're also collecting valuable intel to build a better solution.[19]

I built my Truer Copy Mastermind in response to the success gaps my clients reported from taking other, larger copywriting programs. One of the symptoms of the success gaps I identified was extremely low course completion rates because when a course isn't meeting your needs, you don't stick with it! I made a list of what caused my clients to fail out of those programs and built the structure of my mastermind in response to it. I'm proud to say the completion rate each time I ran my program was 90%—the 10% dropped off only when someone landed in the hospital. For comparison, the average completion rate for big online courses (the only ones currently

---

19 See Chapter 3, "Building Better Offers."

studied) is around 5 to 15%, with a high of 40% for the best ones.[20] Most courses fail more students than they help, but if you can figure out why, you can build your course, program, or service with the support your ideal clients actually need.

Part 4: Why it's hard

They've tried many things but still haven't succeeded, healed, or fixed the issue. Why is this issue so complicated to fix? I call this "the problem under the problem," and it's where you begin to lead the reader through what marketers call "levels of awareness."

Most people are pain-aware or symptom-aware. They know their lower back hurts and they can't crouch down to the lowest kitchen cabinet to grab the biggest, heaviest cast-iron skillet like they used to. Maybe they've tried stretching or taking pain meds, but they're still too stiff to tie their shoelaces in the morning.

There is a root cause of that symptom, and that root cause is why it's not a quick fix.

Maybe they're hypermobile and their overextended hamstrings and tight hip flexors are causing the back pain. Maybe they haven't learned how to work on their core strength, so their joints aren't adequately supported.

This means the solution they really need is NOT more stretching or pain meds that only cover up the symptoms. They need core strengthening exercises and active stretching! (This, incidentally, is why I'm devoted to Pilates.)

---

20 Reich, Justin & Ruipérez-Valiente, José A. (2019). The MOOC pivot. Science. 363. 130-131. 10.1126/science.aav7958. According to Katy Jordan who compiled the MOOC completion databases, the best courses top out at 40% completion.

You're not done because *outside factors* often make problems HARDER to solve.

Like a culture that tells you to "take a pill for it" instead of changing your life for it.

Like corporations that don't allow you control over your work schedule so you can move more and sit less.

Like an industrialized, capitalist medical system that pushes astronomically expensive surgery instead of giving you information about the benefits of mobility exercises and the insurance coverage to pay for a physical therapist, personal trainer, or gym membership.

Like a patriarchal society in which women in pain are often not believed, told to "lose weight" as a cure-all solution, and aren't included in medical studies because their hormones fluctuate throughout the month.

Do you see where I'm going with this? It's important. Your clients are not entirely responsible for their struggles, and those struggles are often not entirely within their ability to fix.

As Sharon Podobnik, author of *It's Not (All) Your Fault*, observes:
"We reduce generations of genetic mutations to a three-step system for losing weight, call our internalization of centuries of structural sexism and racism 'imposter syndrome,' and offer you a meditation to restore the confidence the system destroyed in you." (2022)

Yes, you must take responsibility for yourself and do the best you can because you are a capable human with agency. But you also live in a world that tries to rob you of that agency in a million different ways. This is where ethical copywriting comes in.

If you oversimplify the cause of the problem in your marketing and on your sales page, you set people up to fail with an overly simplistic solution and then blame them (or invite them to blame themselves) for not "trying hard enough" when they still don't succeed. If you don't acknowledge the root causes, you risk perpetuating them.[21] But when you do acknowledge the complexity of the problem, your solution feels more realistic and compassionate.

When you're pondering the wider issues, think societal, cultural, patriarchal, racist, sexist, capitalist, ableist, individualist, or genetic (fill in your favorites). When you take a hard look at the big picture, you're not only going to build offers that help individuals reach their desired outcomes but also educate them and empower them to advocate for themselves and, possibly, create real change on a broader scale.

Nobody says you can (or should) do this on a sales page. But a sales page is the perfect place to sow the seeds of revolution.

When I guide my clients and students to figure out the problems under the problem, I ask them these questions:
1. Examine the surface: What symptoms are your clients aware of right now? What's bugging them, frustrating them, or interfering with their lives that they can readily tell you without thinking very hard?

---

[21] I work in the personal development, spiritual help, and healing niches and there is a pervasive problem among some practitioners of ignoring external factors in favor of believing in—and selling—an absurd amount of individual control. Then, when clients fail to "manifest" wellness, maintain their "high vibe," or manage their trauma in a spiritually enlightened way, they're likely to flagellate themselves for those failures when they don't experience the miraculous cure they were promised.

2. Scratch the surface: What do *you* think is causing those symptoms? Are your clients aware of the cause, or is your point of view going to be an "aha" moment for them?
3. Dig deeper: What has created the conditions for this problem to be so widespread that there is a market for your services? Why do so many people have this problem? Why aren't they able to solve it themselves?
4. Excavate widely: What ideas, stories, worldviews, cultural paradigms are lurking, largely unquestioned, at the base?
5. Are your clients having reasonable reactions to unreasonable demands or circumstances? (Their reactions may not serve them, but I'd bet they're understandable!)
6. Here's the best part of this exercise: As you answer these five questions, you're developing your unique point of view. Your point of view is your most powerful differentiator in a crowded market, which is why I devote a chunk of the sales page to it.

Part 5: Your POV origin story

The solutions or modalities, or combination of techniques, or perspective on what your clients really need to get the outcomes they want—it took you time to develop them. Something happened that sent you on a search for answers. Your search brought you to many places. You tried several ways to fix the issue. You failed and tried again. Then you finally figured it out.

This is where you tell the story of that journey.

How did you find The Way That Works (for you)?

Did your journey start because you experienced the same symptoms and problems as your ideal clients? If so, tell the story of how you discovered the root cause of your symptoms and how you finally healed, improved, or alleviated it. Heck, maybe even accepted it.[22] Be specific about what you tried—what kinds of doctors you sought out, what types of therapy you've had, which modalities you experimented with, what books you read, what podcasts you listened to, which teachers you studied under—and which of these worked, didn't work, or kinda worked.

Don't spend too long here. Think of this as your Rocky Balboa training montage (cue "Eye of the Tiger"). Chug those raw eggs, run up those stairs, wear sweatpants as you sprint through dumpster fires, and then return to the plot.

At some point on this journey, you synthesized all of that information from your lived experience and everything you tried and learned and created a better solution.

The key to writing this as a section on your sales page (rather than as your entire about page) is to keep it short. This isn't about you. It's ultimately about your reader. When they see themselves in your journey, they feel like they know you and might be able to trust you with their journey.

If you're thinking "But I don't share my client's journey! I haven't struggled with their problems," don't worry—I fall under that category, too. So do many photographers, website designers, nutritionists, personal trainers, and so many service-based entrepreneurs making a living off of their innate gifts.

Many of my clients struggle with writing, which I've always

---

22 Selling acceptance is hard. Few people are willing to buy "learn to live with it" until they've tried literally everything else. Writing sales pages for intuitive eating coaches is an interesting challenge for that reason, but when I do, I lean into the POV and the POV origin story sections.

found relatively easy. But, because I've worked with so many clients, I have a lot of experience with their struggles and needs that informs my unique approach.

I can tell the story of the big problem many of my clients face—I frequently see new business owners unable to use their new copy after a few months because their offers and niches change as they rapidly gain experience and clarity. I can also share how that insight led me to develop a unique set of lower-priced offers to help them get over those early-stage hurdles without breaking the bank every time they need updated copy.

A photographer might talk about how their approach puts the client at ease, so they look natural and relaxed. They can describe how they learned to get unposed, yet flattering headshots. Maybe even how they created a hybrid service of body image and confidence coaching with their photography business.

Personal trainers who've always loved fitness can talk about what their clients need to start enjoying workouts and how they've developed training techniques that emphasize joyful movement.

For us, the story is about what we've observed our clients need (and weren't finding elsewhere) and how we've created more effective solutions in response to those needs.

Note: You can use all of this section's material to write your about page, which Chapter 6 covers in depth.

Part 6: The Way That Works

Your discovery journey should naturally end when you find The Way That Works—what you found to be missing, true, and needed to bridge the success gaps[23] left by other methods. Describe how the solution you found worked for you and what you are able to do now. Then, talk about the results you've seen your clients achieve when they try your way.

Part 7: Offer details + CTA + testimonials

Now your reader is ready for the details—more than just the quick Need 2 Knows. Give them enough information to make a confident decision whether or not this is right for them. This may include:

- How you deliver the program (e.g., one-to-one coaching, group program, self-study).
- The program dates and how much time it typically takes to complete.
- A summary of each program module or of what you'll be covering each week.
- A description of what to expect (you can keep this loose; if it varies, just say so).
- Financial commitment and if you offer payment plans.
- What they'll be able to do or have by the end of your time together (or share previous clients' results).[24]
- What guarantee you offer, if any.

---

[23] Success gap: the distance between where your ideal client is now and where they would like to be.
[24] Be careful not to feature "outliers" who've gotten incredible results most people cannot reasonably expect.

You don't have to offer a "money-back guarantee" if you can't afford it or it's not reasonable. I offer an "it's-gotta-work guarantee" for my full-service (most expensive) offers. I can't guarantee my clients' results with the copy I write because too many factors are outside my control (like their entire marketing ecosystem). But I can guarantee I will be there for them, ready to offer feedback and suggestions. What can you reasonably guarantee?

CTA (call-to-action) buttons are their own art form. I like to keep it simple. "Learn More," or "Buy Now," or "Apply Here," or "Book a Call" are sufficient. But there's been a trend among mainstream marketers the last few years to use the CTA as a final pressure point. Often, what they choose to dig into with copy surrounding the CTA button is:

Shame:
- "If you really want to change, sign up now."
- "If you need to think about signing up, you probably don't trust yourself."
- "Do you want to [get X result]? Yes → Show me how or No → I like when [bad thing happens]."[25]

Confirm Shaming:
- For a newsletter, this might look like: "No, I'm not interested in ethical marketing. I'd like to continue doing it dirty."
- For a discount: "No, I don't want to save money. I like being poor."
- For a freebie: "No, I don't want to get better at managing my finances."

---

[25] Pop-up copy from "Choices, Consequences and the Reason Every Pop-Up Box Needs 2 Buttons: Opt In, and Opt Out" by Joanna Wiebe, Copyhackers, 2015

This can go very bad very fast, depending on what you're shaming and what dire consequences you're painting as a result.

A 2024 article on CTAs[26] recommends using them to create a sense of urgency and scarcity (FOMO marketing), provoke emotions, and surround them with "key messages" about "limited-time offers, temporary deals or discounts, or updates on remaining stock availability."

If the scarcity is real, I'm fine with it. But this goes wrong if you use false scarcity and urgency, such as, "This deal goes away in three minutes!" with a countdown timer that forces the reader to decide faster than their logical mind can manage. I've seen this on many product-based websites, but it has crept into service-based websites, too.

Provoking emotions in CTA copy is an interesting gray area when you see it in practice. *Provoking* is inherently manipulative, but is it wrong to say "Join us to be part of the magic" or "Start your adventure today"? I don't think so. Phrases like these excite us. And that's not necessarily a bad idea—after all, often part of what you pay for is excitement, explaining the enduring appeal of Jeeps and Italian sports cars. No judgment from me there—I'd turn in my practical Kia for a vintage Jeep CJ 7 in a hot minute.

Surrounding your CTAs with critical messages, as the article suggests, is a great idea, depending on the messages. Real scarcity? Sure. Real urgency? Okay. Testimonials from other happy clients? Enthusiastic YES.

One fun experiment I've tried is a "Don't Buy Yet" button (it leads to nowhere). This is like snapping your fingers to get someone's attention if they're drifting off behind the wheel because I want readers to snap out of the sales-page lull and think hard before hitting the "buy" button. This is the opposite of using the sheer length of a sales page to wear your reader down. Here, you're waking them up.

---

26 "Top 10 E-Commerce Call-To-Action Best Practices (With Examples)" by Salma Habib, Converted.in, February 22, 2024

> **DON'T BUY YET**

(This is the Don't Buy Yet button. It's here to make sure you know what you're getting into.)

Testimonials

I always pair my CTA buttons with testimonials directly below. I want the support of social proof[27] at the moment someone is seriously considering saying yes. When your readers see someone else who has been successful with the product or service, they think it just might be possible for them, too. Effective testimonials help build trust.

Testimonials are most effective when you have these three components:
1. Photo of the person providing the testimonial
2. Name + business name or job title or where they are in the world
3. Testimonials that speak to the problem they came in with AND what they were able to do after working with you

Getting all three ingredients for each testimonial is surprisingly difficult. Some people will give you a beautiful testimonial but not allow you to use their photo or their name. They have their reasons for

---

[27] One of Robert Cialdini's principles of influence

this; respect them. I keep these partial testimonials in a folder to use later as client-language inspiration. I thank the contributors sincerely, but I do not use these testimonials on my website. No photo? No name? Not much trust there.

The exception to this rule is if your business or clients require anonymity—like attorney-client privilege or confidentiality requirements for therapists. Some business and leadership coaches also have trouble sharing identifiable details in testimonials because their clients could get into trouble at work. In these cases, use the testimonial without names or photos, but explain why identifying details are missing in fine print below. This will still build trust, and your clients will appreciate that their struggles will be treated sensitively.

When asking for testimonials, I create a Google Form (I do almost everything for my business in Google Docs) that asks for feedback on the program or service, then specifically include a short list of questions designed to prompt the contributor to give the most helpful feedback—which will also be a strong testimonial IF they consent to that usage.

The form looks like this:

Hello! Thank you for offering to provide feedback—it's such a GIFT! These questions are just prompts to get you started, but feel free to do your own thing.
Lauren

Which service did I help you with?
- ☐ Copy Coaching
- ☐ Make the Words Go Away
- ☐ Loom Review
- ☐ Other?

1. What drew you to that service? What were you struggling with or hoping for when you found it?
2. Now that you have your new copy, have you noticed that you get more clients, better-fit clients, or both? Please tell me what's happened in your business!
3. What's the most important thing people should know about working with me?
4. Would you recommend me and my services? If so, why and to whom?
5. Anything else you'd like to add?
6. Is there anything you would have liked to see done differently? If so, what?
- May I use your feedback as a testimonial with your name and business publicly displayed?
- If yes, please attach your favorite photo.

Thank you so much—your feedback helps me build better offers, and testimonials mean the world to small businesses like mine.

Ethical considerations when including testimonials:
1. Always get consent to use kind words as a testimonial.
2. Don't use a testimonial given for one offer to support another offer—UNLESS you explicitly state that's what you're doing. Using testimonials for past programs is common when you have a new offer that doesn't have any testimonials yet. This is fine if you are transparent about where the testimonials came from and those testimonials speak to experiences your future clients can expect (like your teaching style).
3. If a client has enjoyed incredible success after your program, but you know it's not *only* due to your program, provide that additional context—"Althea built her copywriting business to six figures within six months, partly due to this program and partially because she had pre-existing industry contacts from 20 years of working in a marketing agency. Here's what she has to say about how this program contributed to her success…" Almost always you contribute to your client's results but are not the sole reason for those results.
4. When choosing testimonials to feature on your sales pages, be careful about the outliers who succeeded to a far greater extent than is typical of most participants. If one person made $3 million in one week after working with you, that's great. But if that doesn't reflect your average client success rate, using it as a "see what you can do!" type of testimonial is ethically questionable. If you do use an outlier, be transparent about it with something like, "Most clients see X results, but one client is now living her best #yachtlife. Your results may vary."

Part 8: Fit check

This is a blunt, bullet-point list of criteria or characteristics that make someone a perfect fit for your offer. There are many different types of fit, and you'll find that the ones you need reveal themselves to you as you work with more people, some of whom you love (what is it about them you enjoy so much?) and some of whom make you wish you'd stayed in a cubicle (what about them drives you up the proverbial wall?).

Until you get your list together, here are some types of fit you may want to include:

1. Problem/solution fit: Do they have the problem you solve, and do you have the kind of solution they need?
2. Experience fit: Do you offer the container (or experience) they need to succeed? For example, a self-study program works well for people who can make the time to sit and study regularly without accountability (very few people can, by the way). That won't work for someone who excels with one-to-one attention or who craves the support of a group of like-minded people. It's not just about what your clients learn—it's about how they learn best.
3. Values fit: If you can't imagine working with someone who has values (or political views or philosophies) that differ significantly from yours, be clear about it. I will not work with multi-level marketing businesses or weight-loss-focused dieticians (for similar reasons, now that I think about it). You're not here to make friends with everyone, so be fearless about stating where you stand so your people can find you.
4. Knowledge fit: If they need to be at a particular stage of

their business (or a certain age, life stage, level of professional or life experience) to succeed with you, let them know. Many copywriters only want to work with mid-to-advanced-level business owners because they already know their niche and messaging. Me? I love working with the newer business owners who are still figuring it out.

5. Philosophical fit: This can cover a lot of ground, but essentially, it's your ideas on how the world works, what has gone wrong, and what your people need. It could also be your take on the state of the world, how things should be, or your take on right and wrong. If your approach is rooted in a spiritual practice or faith, make sure you say so to filter out anyone who isn't open to it.

6. Technology fit: Believe me, you do not want to be tech support if that is not your primary offer! So if you use Zoom, Google Docs, Voxer, or Slack—or prefer the old-fashioned phone call—be clear that they must be comfortable on those platforms (or can find help).

7. Time fit: What time commitment does the work require of your clients? What does this look like in a day, week, month, or longer? Can you help them visualize it by setting up a calendar graphic and blocking out the time? You'll get fewer "flakes" if you ask them to verify that they do have the time (or admit that they don't). It can also help if you explain why their best chance at success requires this amount of time investment.

Part 9: Fear Soother Section (FAQs)

"Frequently asked questions" tends to be a misnomer for small businesses. Unless you've been in business a while, you likely don't have the volume of prospects or clients to get frequently asked questions! So instead, I want you to think of this as the "Fear Soother Section" where you predict what might be causing right-fit clients to hesitate and answer the questions surfacing in their minds. Do not confuse this with "handling objections." You are answering legitimate questions your prospects might have.

Most fears people have before committing to buy are around four core questions:
1. Will this work for me?
2. Can I afford it?
3. Do I have time for it?
4. Will this require me to do something scary, painful, or against my values?

"Will this work for me?" should be answered with an "if/then" statement.
"If [the fit check] is true, and you're willing and able to do the work, then yes, this will likely work for you. I can't promise results, but past clients have been able to do [list reasonable results], and a couple were even able to do [greatest-hits results]."

"Can I afford it?" is actually asking about payment plans (or a sliding scale), maybe even scholarships. In what ways do you make your offer financially accessible?

"Do I have time for it?" often comes up as "I have another commitment at X time" or "I live in a different time zone, and the group call is at 3 a.m." They want to know if they can miss a call to pick up their kid from school and still get the full benefit of the offer. For some types of offers, your answer may be yes (they can watch a recording), and for other offers, your answer may be no (they do have to be there). I like to build flexibility into my offers by recording calls and provide enough structure for accountability with makeup calls or co-working sessions at different times.

"Is this going to require me to do something scary, painful, or against my values?" can show up as all kinds of questions, from "Is this witchcraft? Are you worshiping the Devil?" to "I'm concerned that dredging up memories will retraumatize me. Are you trauma-informed?" The answer will involve how you create a safe, supportive container for the hard work.

Sometimes, people will ask you if there is a guarantee. This rarely happens. But if it does, it may be a red flag that someone is trying to find a way out of paying you. Let's assume they're on the up and up; how do you answer this question?

The answer to "Can you guarantee a result?" is almost always no. But when they ask this question, they really want to know how you will support them so they have the best possible chance at getting their desired outcome. Discuss what support and accountability you offer and what happens if shit hits the fan and they can't complete the program.

The last time I offered my group program, I offered a "shit happens" guarantee to provide student support after the course completed should their life blow up (e.g., someone lands in the hospital, someone close dies, or someone gets diagnosed with something scary). Incidentally, at least one of these has happened for at least one person EVERY time I've run this program. One of those times, it was *my* life that blew up when my father passed unexpectedly in the middle of the course. That's why I always give my students more support and grace. We all need it sometimes.

One final thought:

On your sales page, it's your responsibility to support, promote, and encourage your readers to engage in critical thinking and the ability to make decisions and judgment calls for themselves. Use your copy and sales processes to position them (rather than you) as the ultimate authority on what they need. Sure, show them the way that worked for you, but empower them to make the best decision for them. This is the heart of ethical copywriting.

Takeaways

1. **Lead with transparency:** Include a clear "Need to Knows" section at the top of your page. Clearly displaying important details like pricing and time commitment builds trust. Empower your readers with the information they need to decide for themselves.
2. **Avoid "pain point" manipulation:** Use empathy, not agitation. Describe your reader's situation with understanding and avoid "punching the bruise."
3. **Highlight what they've already tried:** Show them you understand their journey by listing specific approaches they may have tried before coming to you.
4. **Offer your unique perspective:** Briefly share the "origin story" of your solution, letting your readers in on your philosophy and what makes your approach different.
5. **Use honest CTAs:** Skip guilt-tripping phrases or false urgency. Trust your reader to decide without extra pressure.
6. **Filter for right-fit clients:** Outline exactly who your offer is for. This saves both you and the reader from misalignment.
7. **Address legitimate questions in the FAQs:** Use this section to answer real concerns, not to "handle objections." Aim to calm, not convince.

CHAPTER 6

How to Talk About Yourself (and Why You Should)

When I could finally afford professional website design, I was so excited. I'm a bit of a design fangirl and working with a creative designer to bring my business to visual life was a longtime wish. So there I was, in front of my computer, with 50 tabs open on the screen, each one a different website designer. That day, I realized how important about pages are when hiring a service provider.

Follow my "buyer's journey"[28] for a minute: I found 50 website designers who specialized in my preferred platform and clicked on each of their websites. The first page I landed on was the home page for each one. If I liked their design aesthetic, I clicked on their about page. Not their services page, not their sales page—their about page.

I didn't want to hire just any designer. I wanted to hire someone who could translate the feel of working with me into visual branding. Someone to help me figure out which colors, fonts, and layouts would best reflect my personality and how I wanted my clients to feel (cozy, held, seen, safe). I also needed someone who would rein in my maximalist tendencies. Most importantly, I needed to feel like

---

28 The "buyer's journey" is a marketing term for how a new buyer, or client, finds you and decides to buy from you. It encompasses the stages of awareness (problem aware, solution aware, product aware) and every touchpoint the buyer experiences when encountering your brand, from the first ad they see to messaging they receive even after purchasing.

they would "get" my quirky, multi-passionate nature rather than try to cover it with trendy greige.[29] I scanned each about page and had several epiphanies that guide my work to this day:

1. The about pages that were clearly written with "copywriting best practices" and were more about the reader than the designer turned me off. These pages all led with pain points like sales pages almost always do. As I scrolled through, I thought, "You understand my problem? Cool. So do I. I came to this page to learn about YOU, not me." This flew in the face of everything I'd been taught and had taught others: The about page is not about you, the business owner; it's about your clients (so you should start the page talking about them). I've since altered how I write and teach about pages to lean more toward telling the business owner's story and developing their point of view.

2. The most compelling about pages showed me who the designer was as a person by including their interests, hobbies, taste in literature, pets, and favorite TV shows. Their interests didn't have to match mine for me to identify with them. For example, I love hanging out with Trekkies (Star Trek fans) even though I don't identify as one because we share that streak of essential nerdiness. These small bites of information are known as "Fun facts" and are typically an afterthought, or considered optional. They shouldn't be. They are selling points.

3. The weirdness in me honors the weirdness in you. Bland about pages that were purely professional did not make the cut. If I wanted a website design that felt authentic, I

---

29 Greige: a blend of gray and beige that has been on trend in minimalist website design for years.

wanted to work with someone who wasn't afraid to put their authentic self on their website. For me, the weirder[30] the better.

Now, my approach to teaching how to write about pages is more of a balance between showing how well you understand your clients' problems and who you are—because that second part matters just as much. I encourage my clients to tell their unvarnished stories, show up fully, and be fearless.

That said… I have seen A LOT of about page drafts as a copywriter and copywriting instructor for two excellent entrepreneurship programs. I host workshops on how to write about pages at least four times a year because this page is the hardest, and there are so many counterintuitive ways it can go wrong.

Before we go into each potential pitfall, let's review the goal of the about page.

The goal of the about page is to answer one question in your reader's mind:
Are you the person I want to guide me through this?

You can think of it like this: The home page answers "what?" (what is this? Is this what I need?), the about page answers "who?" (is this the person I want to work with?), and the sales page answers "how?" (how will we work together? How will you help me succeed?).

A considerable part of answering the "who?" question is telling your story in a way that makes readers feel like they know you, like you,

---

30 I know some people bristle at the word "weird," but I identify with it. I've always felt like the weird kid, and it's never felt like a bad thing.

and trust you.[31] This is where you enter hard mode.

Pitfall #1: You're just too close

First, writing your about page is like licking your elbow: You're just too close. When you're trying to write about yourself, it's personal. You're emotionally attached to the story. You want to tell it accurately, chronologically, and perhaps fudge unflattering facts. Or you veer in the other direction: Keep it business-only with few details that allow the reader to get to know you (which reads like a resume). The worst part is that as a DIY writer, you're rarely aware when you're verging on too much information or too little or if you're including the right information your readers need to connect with you.

The about page becomes much easier when you stop thinking about it like it's your autobiography, success story, manifesto, or (worse) resume. It's not any of those things, but it may include elements of all of those things.

When teaching the about page, I've called it "your secret sales page" to help students think of it as anything BUT their autobiographies. However, I want you to be careful about this. When you treat the about page as just another sales tool, it becomes tempting only to tell the parts of your story and philosophy you think will make people want to buy. It works better to think of it as a "personality fit" page or a philosophy page. You're doing it right as long as your page answers the "are you the *person* I want to guide me through this?" question. And you will likely do this by writing the story of how you found the way you now help your ideal clients. I call this the point of view origin story.

---

31   Cialdini, Robert B. Influence, New and Expanded: The Psychology of Persuasion. New York: HarperCollins, 2021.

Pitfall #2: Storytelling can be used to manipulate or connect

You will be using storytelling techniques from the NLP chapter, which, as we've seen, can be used to manipulate. But they can also be used to meaningfully connect. That fine line is determined by honesty, authenticity, and intention, which is all that stands between you and using this page to charm readers into buying from you.

There are two storylines you'll often see in about pages which can be problematic:
The rock-bottom to success story
The six-figure corporate job to dream business story

Both usually carry the undercurrent of "I am the expert, and I have it all figured out. This is my success story, and you can have it too!"
That is not a problem if it's true. But it is a problem when it's not the whole story. If you don't talk about how many hours you're putting into your dream business and how many sacrifices you make (little sleep, less time for friends and family, no time for hobbies or outside interests), you're selling a pipedream. If you're making your version of success look easier than it is by not addressing your privilege, the systemic inequalities you've had to overcome, or the sacrifices you've made that cost dearly, you are not writing in service to your readers. You're manipulating them.
Think of the fitness influencer who spends every waking moment counting calories yet promises "five-minute abs" from a workout.
Think of the business coach who quit her six-figure job, only to make multiple six figures in her business (marrying an investment banker who supported her for the first year while she figured it out but who is never mentioned).

To write an ethical about page, share your story with vulnerability, honesty, and acknowledgment of the difficulties, sacrifices, and time spent getting to where you are. And if you don't have all the answers, it's okay to say so.

Just don't *dwell* on what you don't know or what you weren't able to do because that can undermine your credibility. I've had many leadership and life coach clients tell me, "I don't have the answers. My clients have all the answers they need inside of them!" And I reply, "That's great, but they're not going to pay you for what they already have. Let's focus on what you help them do!" Even if your story isn't perfect, or doesn't come with the "happily ever after" ending you help your clients achieve, focus on the value you have to offer.

Pitfall #3: Writing your success story instead of the real story

One of my students was struggling to write her about page because her story didn't fit the usual mold. She asked: "What if my story doesn't wrap up in a neat ending? What if I didn't get the results I'm helping others get? Should I make it up?"

This pitfall happens when you assume your about page is your success story. It isn't.

Should you lie? No. Never. Should you stretch the truth into a more palatable version to make a sale? No. Never.

Remember, you are building legitimate know, like, and trust. That means being trustworthy and transparent, especially when your story doesn't tie neatly into a bow. I love it when someone's story is more "complicatedly ever after" than "happily ever after." My suggestion to that student was to write what really happened, what she learned from it, and how it informed her approach with her clients.

Instead of happily ever after, it was *complicatedly ever after*, which is much more effective at building trust and connection.

My favorite example of "complicatedly ever after" was a client who specialized in coaching men and women to soften their defensiveness, stop pushing love away, and find their forever partners. Her journey began with trying to find love and working on herself to enter into a healthy, loving relationship when and if it materialized. But it didn't materialize even after she'd done the work! She was honest about it and showed all the benefits she got from doing the work anyway. Here is an excerpt from her about page.

> *My journey began with a single focus: getting myself ready to be in a relationship. I was truly excited about what I was discovering about myself and the life I was cultivating, but somewhere in the midst of becoming, a relationship stopped being my focus.*
>
> *I've cultivated new friendships and made peace with old, toxic friendships. I was able to re-engage with people I love with healthy, well-established boundaries. I have a healthy dating life now (and I don't try to turn sex into marriage anymore!). I get to know people based on my values and figure out where I want them to fit in MY life. And I don't fall apart if I'm rejected.*
>
> *At work, I changed how I showed up energetically, too. I stopped acting defensive and isolating myself, got three promotions, and increased my salary by nearly 50% in five years.*
>
> *I'm not perfect. My life isn't utopia. Growth is an everyday struggle. But I found peace and love of self. And it feels good to finally bloom.*[32]

---

[32] Written by Lauren Van Mullem for Aurelia Gardner, unpublished website copy draft, 2021.

Honesty sells better than inflated or false outcomes because it promotes trust. An old saying is, "Don't let the truth get in the way of a good story." But my advice is: Don't let a good story get in the way of the truth.

Pitfall #4: Presenting a "more marketable" self that isn't you at all

We all want to be the heroes of our stories, put our best feet forward, and airbrush the metaphorical wrinkles of our backstories, but a perfect persona doesn't connect (or sell) as well as being yourself.

Several years ago, a gruff, curt, and critical writing coach came to me. She didn't seem to like *people*, much less her clients. I would have been terrified to hire her (I say I take criticism well, but like most writers, I'm a sensitive flower). When writing her about page, I was tempted to soften the rougher edges of her personality, but when I read through her testimonials and client feedback, I changed my mind.

Her clients loved her honest feedback and expertise. They didn't want to be coddled, and if they received praise, they knew they'd earned it. Clearly, she wasn't trying to charm anyone into working with her. So I leaned into it and made sure her personality was infused into the language of that page. I took extensive, verbatim notes on our calls and focused on her philosophy of what made good writing. I included a little of what it was like to work with her (stressing her no-nonsense approach). Most importantly, I used her exact words from my notes to write the page. It became a highly effective filter that helped her bring in more clients who appreciated her style and made sure she didn't "waste her time" on the rest. *Her words, not mine.*

I've also been guilty of trying to present a more marketable version of myself in my own business. When I first changed my niche to coaches and healers, I created a Pinterest board of images so I could study what the well-known coaches wore, how they did their hair, and how they posed for the camera. The whole board was filled with women wearing ripped jeans and cozy sweaters, with freshly blown-out hair, carrying a mug in one hand and a laptop in the other while sitting on the floor barefoot in front of a perfectly good couch. You will see versions of that exact photo everywhere once you start noticing it.

So I did that. I got my hair done, bought new ripped jeans and a sweater, and paid a professional photographer to take pictures of me sitting on the floor in front of perfectly serviceable furniture. My website, with the new photos, was okay. I brought in some clients. But my business only took off when I shed every nonsense idea of how I *should* look to attract coaching clients and was just myself. Fast forward a couple of years to when my husband took pictures of me in my favorite vintage clothes in our own backyard, snacking on blackberries and hanging out with the chickens. I can't tell you how many clients tell me, "As soon as I saw that picture of you with the chicken, I knew you were the one."

The moral here is this: If you're an introvert, be an introvert. If you're grouchy, be a grouch. If you're high vibes and angel blessings, shine bright. If you're a raging feminist, embrace beast mode. Don't be afraid to bring your real self to your business, especially on your about page. Your right-fit clients will love you for it.

Pitfall #5: Too much information

When I say "bring your real self" and tell the "whole story," there's an art to it. Because if you take me literally, you may write your entire autobiography, which is not in service to your readers either. TMI tends to stem from two issues:

1. You contain multitudes, and writing about yourself can feel like cramming the entire Brady Bunch into a studio apartment.
2. Your background has serious rough patches that are personal and painful. You're not sure how much to share.

As a multi-passionate business owner who identifies strongly with ADHD content on TikTok (read: undiagnosed neurodivergent), I've found that people like me tend to struggle with TMI because we have so much going on. When I have to write about myself, the question that springs to mind is, "Which self?"

Some people do not have this problem. My husband, for example, has one solid identity. At most, he has a "work self" and a "home self," but that's where the variety ends. He'd have a very easy time writing his about page. I can't imagine being that cohesive.

I have to take the extra step of deciding which facets of myself to show because all of them would be overwhelming and confusing. For example, I enjoy mixed martial arts, axe throwing, Scotch, and occasional Cuban cigars. But I also love tea, vintage dresses, gardening, and snuggling with any creature with fur or feathers who'll let me. Both together? Picture Ron Swanson from *Parks and Rec* sipping Scotch from a teacup while wearing a dress and petting a chicken. CONFUSING.

When I first switched niches and took my branding seriously, I tried to create a "brand personality" that would appeal to the coaches I wanted to work with. That was a mistake. I was trying to look, dress, and act like what I saw in coach-world. It didn't work at all because it wasn't me.

I only started to attract the clients I love when I created a brand that felt like an extension of my Truest Self. My core personality, passions, values, and my love for plants, animals, and tea.

Our businesses only work if we are authentic—but not confusing. For me, my answer was to curate a brand that is 100% true to me but isn't 100% all of me.

Here's how I curated it:

I asked myself, What version of me best supports my clients?

My answer: The tea-drinking, ultra-empathetic, gardening, animal nurturing, quirky/nerdy version. Because I want to create a safe place for my clients to get vulnerable and feel supported.

I left a lot on the cutting room floor, but my essential self is there.

Here are some questions that can help guide your curation:
1. What do you do to make your clients feel supported?
2. How do you put your clients at ease?
3. What values guide your everyday actions?
4. What interests or hobbies do you share with your clients, or if not shared, what can they relate to?
5. What do you struggle with, personally or professionally? This can be something profound or silly (like chaotically loading the dishwasher and feeling annoyed when your spouse silently reorganizes it—just me?)

The goal is not to use those questions as a template, but as a compass. Keep the answers to these questions in the back of your mind as you write the story of how you became the business owner you are today.

We're entering fine-line territory again here. Curating, pruning, or selecting parts of your story to share with the goal of being of service to the reader is fine. Falsifying information or conveniently leaving out parts of your story to sell an Instagram-worthy lifestyle is not.

What if the story of becoming the business owner you are today includes sensitive material?

Some clients ask me how much of their stories they should tell—often because their stories are intensely personal, painful, triggering, or so shocking or unusual that they beg credulity. My answer is always this: Are you comfortable sharing it, and will sharing it serve your readers?

If you're uncomfortable sharing part of your story, don't. It's your story. You always have that right.

Many of my clients are healers who pursue that path because of their own struggle and wounding. Their stories include trauma from the ugliest parts of humanity and may include wonders, miracles, and experiences that defy scientific explanation. When writing their about pages, I ask them:

- Are you comfortable sharing this part of the story?
- Would your ideal client identify with this part of your story? Would it help them feel seen or less alone?
- Have your clients had similar experiences, or do they hold similar beliefs?

If the answer to any or all of these questions is "no," then that part of the story doesn't make the cut.

But if your hesitation is, "Does this make me sound unhinged?" my answer might surprise you. If your story involves angels, aliens, spirit guides, visions, or prophetic dreams, it won't sound "unhinged" if your ideal clients are right there with you. If that's the case, go ahead and write about it. But, if you're talking about channeling the voice of the universe to your conservative, church-going family, I make no guarantees as to what they'll think.

If your story includes a "rock bottom" you feel ashamed of or that you worry will make you sound unprofessional, untrustworthy, or the target of judgment—let me offer you this: If you are helping people out of the same or similar hard place, they will value your experience. And most people will be impressed at your resilience, rather than judgy.

Pitfall #6: You write your autobiography

The about page is about you, but it's not your autobiography. I teach it as the origin story of your point of view: why you do what you do in the unique way you do it. There is a reason you work with clients the way you do, a history of how you found your modality, and your opinion based on observations of why your system works where others fail. Write that story.

It may be that your own struggles led you to the modality you now use or the solution you help others find. In this case, you'll likely have direct experience with the struggles your ideal clients are working through now. By telling your story, you're holding up a mirror of their story, giving them a hopeful window into the future.

But you may not share your ideal clients' backstory. My clients struggle with writing, which has never been my battle. So the story I tell is how I developed a suite of services that serve new business owners better because they're responsive to early-stage needs and changes. I'm one of the few copywriters to specialize in newer business owners who don't have everything figured out yet, and my journey of learning how to help them best is my POV origin story. And then, I pack it with fun facts and photos of chickens.

The information I find worthwhile to share on my about page is:
1. Shorthand "get to know me" facts like my astrology sign, enneagram number, human design, and main hobbies.
2. My point of view or philosophy, including how I

developed the unique ways I work with clients and how my approach benefits them. Plus, a tiny blurb about my professional experience (harsh truth: nobody cares[33]) and how that background informs my philosophy now.
3. The tidbit I thought was "too weird" to put on my about page and what I do when I'm not writing (I dabble in *a lot* of interests).

If you put that into a formula, it becomes a point-of-view sandwich, with fun facts as the bread and point of view as the satisfying filling. This is an effective and simple structure to use when you don't share your ideal clients' backstory. If you do, you'll need a more robust structure, which I've included at the end of the chapter.

You don't have to be quirky, have a boatload of interests, own a flock of chickens, or list your astrology signs—those just work well for me. But the about page only functions as a filter to bring in your ideal clients when *you do you*. Just be sure to tell the story of how you developed your approach clearly and you'll be fine.

---

33 Nobody cares about your credentials, training, or education UNLESS you get referrals from doctors or lawyers or your ideal clients are Ivy League graduates. The vast majority of clients do.not.care. Really.

ABOUT PAGE OUTLINE

The headline: This can be your warm welcome or an empathy statement that lets them know you "get" where they are.

The intro: "Hi, I'm [your name], and I help [ideal client descriptor] do [hard thing] so they can [get rad result]."

The symptom (or symptoms): you had, that your ideal clients have now. You started this journey because something wasn't working in your life or work—describe that time and how you became aware of the problem.

The search for answers: what you tried, what partially worked, and what didn't work. You searched for answers in all the usual places (list them out and acknowledge that your ideal client has probably tried those, too). You found those solutions were missing something when they didn't solve (or entirely solve) the symptoms.

The real problem or underlying cause of the symptoms: sometimes a bigger truth (i.e., what's wrong with our approach as a society). This explains why it's so hard for people to get results independently.

The Way That Works: This is the solution you finally found and an explanation of why it works better than other solutions. Often, there's a missing element in other approaches, a success gap that other methods fail to bridge.

The after: Whether it's happily ever after, or complicatedly ever after, you are now able to do something you weren't able to before. With the knowledge, skills, and tools you now have, how is your life different? And what are you able to help your clients achieve?

The logical next step or CTA: This typically appears toward the bottom of the page because after they've read your story, your readers will (hopefully) feel inspired to deepen the relationship with you. How would you like them to do that? Sign up for your newsletter? Download your freebie? Book a free first session? Schedule a call? Check out your services page? Make this a big, bright button.

The you behind your business (aka fun facts): This may include what you value, what you do when you're not working (hobbies, interests, funny anecdotes), family, preferred beverages, personality shorthands, what drives you crazy, and what you're a passionate nerd about.

Oh, one last pitfall: Don't make your fun facts braggy or boring. Use self-deprecating humor to prevent accomplishments from sounding braggy. It's the difference between "I've traveled to over 100 countries!" and "I've traveled to over 100 countries and only shat my pants in 60 of them." And if boring is a concern, just add specifics. It's the difference between "I like reading" and "I have a stack of five books on my nightstand, plus a Kindle, and at least two audiobooks going at any given time. The ones I keep coming back to are *Braiding Sweetgrass* and *Tiny Beautiful Things*." Ultimately, these details are points for potential connection. Specificity, humility, and humor are the keys to making them work.

Takeaways

1. **The about page is a personality fit test:** Your about page answers the critical questions: "Are you the person I want to guide me?" and "Are we a fit?"
2. **Blend your story and your client's needs:** While understanding your clients' problems is essential, showing your authentic self and sharing your POV origin story are equally important.
3. **Be honest and transparent:** Share your real story, including challenges and sacrifices. Avoid over-smoothing or embellishing to create a false narrative. You can curate, but keep it real.
4. **Fun facts are selling points:** Include personal interests, hobbies, or quirks to help readers connect with you as a person.
5. **Avoid autobiographical overload:** Focus on the origin story of your unique approach, not your entire life history. Keep it relevant to your audience.
6. **Fearlessly put your authentic self on the page:** Whether you're quirky, introverted, or no-nonsense, infuse your personality into your about page to attract right-fit clients. If you struggle to write the way you speak, you may need to hire a professional who can put the feel of working with you into words. It's hard to do for yourself, even if you enjoy writing.
7. **Storytelling builds trust, but don't sell an incomplete success story:** Don't just share the Instagrammable parts of your ever after. Be real about what it took to get where you are. Also, be real about where you are. I can't tell you the number of "multiple six-figure business owners" who

have struggled to pay me over the years…

8. **TMI is confusing, and confused readers don't buy:** Balance personal sharing with relevance to your audience. It's easy to accidentally overwhelm or confuse readers, especially if you're a complicated, contradictory, multifaceted person (aren't we all?).
9. **Point of view is the main event, but don't forget the side dishes:** Try a "point-of-view sandwich" that begins and ends with relatable fun facts and puts your POV origin story in the middle.

CHAPTER 7

Not-So-Free Freebies and Other Thinly Veiled Sales Pitches

If you have a strong home page that tells your ideal clients "Hey, you're in the right place!" by clearly stating what you do, who it's for, and what it helps them do—then their next logical step is to want to get to know you better. Maybe they'll pop over to your about page. And if they like what they see, they may be ready to buy…but they might not. They might be your ideal client, but they don't have the funds right now or they aren't ready to commit to the journey you're going to take them on. So they sign up for your "freebie"—aka "lead magnet"—to learn about your point of view and keep you on their radar until they're ready.

Freebies can do a lot for your business if they're good. They can be accessible vehicles to introduce your perspective, build relationships and trust, give prospects a window into how it feels to work with you, and can be easily and enthusiastically shared, maximizing your organic reach.

Most importantly, a good freebie can make your reader want to get to know you more and maybe even hire you. But most of the discussion about freebies is limited to using them to "build your list!" Your email list, that is. And that's where we get into ethical difficulties.

There is one GIANT inherent problem with a "freebie"—they're not free. To get the PDF, quiz results, webinar, or "toolkit," you have to hand over your email address. (And for product-based companies, I'm seeing an increasing number of "get 10% off" offers that require you to give them your email address AND your phone number for texts. No, thanks!)

When the name "free" itself is a lie, the ethical choice is easy.

Make it actually free. Ungated. No email required.

And then, when you deliver it, tell them it is an actually-free freebie, explain that they are not automatically dumped onto your email list, and *invite* them to sign up for your newsletter if they would like to deepen their relationship with you.

Here's the paragraph I add to all of my actually-free freebies:

Grab a cup of tea and join me

Oh, hey! This freebie does <u>NOT</u> dump you into my email list (it's an actually-free freebie). So if you'd like to keep in touch, learn about my take on ethical copywriting, and hear about my favorite books, podcasts, and occasional offers, you can sign up here.

<u>Join My Newsletter!</u>

If you've been indoctrinated into the freebie funnel model, you might be experiencing palpitations at this point.

"But I need those email addresses to grow my list!"

You will still build your list with your freebie, but you will do it with transparency and consent. The result may be slower list growth, but a steep increase in the engagement of your leads and future sales.

However, the key to this working is how much value you actually deliver with that freebie.

So many freebies make big promises but are total fluff (i.e., not useful, not actionable, don't deliver any tangible result, and don't offer any truly original ideas).

Useless freebies are a real problem, and you probably have a dozen cluttering up your hard drive right now that you've never even read. Creating useless freebies doesn't help your business because they damage your credibility and erode trust in your ability to provide value. If you use a fluffy freebie to build your list without consent, you'll have high numbers of subscribers who mark your emails as spam. If you use a fluffy freebie to build your list *with* consent, it just won't work.

Useless freebies tend to be:
- Generic PDFs that yield no actionable advice. If you have a freebie that includes the words "why" or "learn about," you are probably guilty of this. Think in terms of "how to" instead.
- AI-generated content. People want your expertise, not a bot's. If you struggle with grammar, use AI to edit it, but make sure the ideas are yours.
- Challenges, workshops, or workbooks that demand too much time (or printed paper) of participants. Keep your freebie long enough to be useful but short enough to avoid overwhelm.
- Quizzes. You'll build a big list fast with a quiz because everyone loves a quiz. But that's the problem: *Everyone* loves a quiz. You'll be paying for an inflated list of uninterested subscribers who never read your emails or buy from you. That said, I have seen website designers and

branding experts use quizzes effectively as the first step toward working together because quizzes *can* help people gain insights into themselves and their preferences that they'll use later when they work with you.

The challenge is to create a genuinely valuable, interesting, accessible, and engaging freebie.

How to create a genuinely great freebie

1. **Help them with the first step toward their goal** Think about what will give your ideal clients a taste of what it's like to work with you, that demonstrates your expertise and delivers tangible value. Where are they trying to go, what are they trying to do, and how can you help them take the first step toward that goal? Just the first step though. Don't overwhelm them or overdeliver. You don't need to hand out your entire program.
2. **Deliver a tangible outcome** Include ideas they can put into practice immediately and experience real progress, but keep them bitesized. You could offer two-minute exercises that build on each other to create clarity. You could offer a five-day challenge of 10-minute morning routines. Keep it tiny and tangible.
3. **Make it fun** If it's not fun, nobody will do it. How can you make the experience intrinsically rewarding? You don't have to include games (or gamification) to make a fun freebie. You can make your freebie visually colorful and exciting, add humor or animal photos, or deliver a cozy POV piece to read with a cup of tea or listen to on a walk. You'll have to think outside of the box, or inbox, to bring

a sense of play to your freebie. And if "fun" is too much to ask, at least make it interesting.
4. **Consider accessibility** How much time do your people have to consume your freebie? What format would make it easier for them to consume? PDFs often aren't effective even if they're packed with actionable tips because nobody wants to sit down to read a PDF. Limited series podcasts, however, can be packed with information and listened to while folding laundry or walking the dog. Other accessibility considerations are to make sure written content is screen-reader-friendly, that videos have captions, and that your font choices are easy to read for those with impaired vision (sans serif, clear spacing, high contrast).
5. **Be generous** The most effective freebies are so surprisingly generous that they get people talking about them and sharing them. The freebie that built my business was giving away one free page of copy per person (your freebie doesn't have to be sustainable; mine has changed over time as my business has grown and my time has shrunk).

Eight types of freebies I've seen work well

There are so many types of freebies you can offer and it's really fun to come up with creative gifts that are unique to your business. Some of my favorite freebies I've done, and seen my clients use, are:
1. **Monthly moon circles:** An online-group call that offers a simple ritual or reading and getting-to-know-you time. This type of freebie builds relationships and engagement well.
2. **Monthly "ask me anything" call:** I do this, but I call it a

"Craft 'n Copy Hour" call where people can bring a copy question and/or a craft they're working on and listen to me answer questions while I knit. It's so cozy. This type of freebie allows you to demonstrate your expertise while building relationships in an informal setting.

3. **Free coaching session** (aka gift session[34]): A real full-length session that is all about the prospective client and does not turn into a sales call. You can invite them to book a second call where you just talk about working together, but the gift session is 100% value, 0% pitch. This type of freebie demonstrates value and expertise and serves as a final fit check.

4. **Free challenge:** Whether it's a week of tidying one tiny corner of your house each day[35] or a 30 days of yoga.[36] You can use automated emails and/or pre-recorded content for this, which is an added bonus for busy business owners. This type of freebie is fun, engaging, and easy for people to share.

5. **Free review:** If part of your work involves helping your clients improve what they have, offer a free, short review (of their niche, website, brand photography, offers, whatever your specialty is). I've seen these go from 60-second niche reviews on Instagram[37] to a 15-minute Loom review of home page copy (one of my previous experiments). This type of freebie demonstrates value and expertise.

6. **Limited-series podcast:** Record a limited set of audio

---

34 Business coach Caroline Leon strongly advocates for gift sessions, especially for newer coaches, and has written about them extensively on her website: www.carolineleon.com.
35 Katherine North's "Queen Sweep" challenge
36 Yoga with Adriene
37 One of Tad Hargrave's freebie experiments for Marketing for Hippies

files people can listen to as a "podcast." When you have a strong point of view or just have a lot to say on your subject, plan three to five 20-minute episodes where you share what you really think. It's fun, valuable, and accessible for people with limited time because they can listen to you while folding laundry. This type of freebie is ideal to showcase your expertise and unique point of view. It can also help prospects decide if working with you feels like a fit.

7. **Templates or swipe files:** Show them exactly how to do something or write something and then give them a folder of inspiration. You can do one or both, but I like how they support each other. This type of freebie is accessible, actionable, and delivers great value.

8. **Free workshop:** Share something immediately actionable and useful. You can host this yourself or you can offer it as a "signature workshop" to memberships and groups. I love hosting workshops for private groups because I can experiment with ideas (like writing copy based on the enneagram) in a low-stakes way while introducing more people to my work. This type of freebie is great for expanding your reach in specific communities when you guest host.

Be aware that there is a psychological effect at play here. When you give someone something for free, the principle of reciprocity[38] will make the recipient feel obligated to give something of value in return. In fact, they're even more likely to respond this way when you make it clear there are no strings attached. You're creating a level of discomfort if they feel like they owe you, and people take action to move away from pressure. That action might be subscribing to your list.

---

38 Cialdini, Robert B. Influence. 5th ed., Pearson, 2008.

This is how human brains work, and as ethical marketers, we need to be aware of it and avoid taking advantage of it (by delivering value without strings and appreciating fair exchange when it happens but not expecting or demanding it).

But wait! There's another ethical way to build your email list...

You don't have to lure readers in with your freebie and hope they choose to subscribe… You can lead with simply asking your website visitors to join your newsletter. And THEN shower them with gifts afterward.

I've done this both ways, and both ways work because they prioritize consent and transparency and ensure your list grows with genuinely interested readers. Here's what it looks like when you lead with the invitation to subscribe first.

On my home page, I use the header section to invite readers to my newsletter and *then* they get my Ethical Copywriting Starter Kit. Here is the call-to-action copy:

Grab a cup of tea and join me

Subscribe to my newsletter and get your Ethical Copywriting Starter Kit! The essential elements of every page to bring in more ideal clients without manipulation.

[First Name]   [Email Address]

Let's make your inbox a little more cozy.

The difference between this invitation and the traditional lead magnet is that I'm asking them to subscribe first and then saying "Oh, you'll also get this useful kit." The traditional way would be "Want a free starter kit? Enter your email address!" (which then dumps the person—who only wanted the kit—into a sales funnel they never asked for).

My starter kit sequence is not exactly a sales funnel, though I do highlight free and paid ways to get support when it makes sense. It's more of a *philosophy funnel* to introduce my readers to some ethical copywriting fundamentals they can start using immediately. This gives them the chance to decide if my approach resonates with them…or not.

The newsletter experience starts with a welcome page that tells new subscribers what to expect in the next two weeks, offers a hefty discount code (note: I don't even mention the discount code *before* someone subscribes—I want an engaged audience, not deal hunters!), and three popular workbooks they might want to buy (now that they have that discount).

The next six emails look like this:

Email 1 is where I introduce myself, my values, my take on ethical copywriting, and set expectations for the next five emails in the series and my regular newsletter after that.

Email 2 is the first starter kit email and includes my top three tips for an ethical home page and a gift template for a one-page website (this is a surprise), an invitation to my free Craft 'n Copy Hour, and a link to one of my favorite Truer Business Podcast episodes (fun and cozy!).

Email 3 delivers three tips for an ethical sales page, a cute cat photo, and a video of me performing a dramatic reading of my favorite sales page intro, followed by another invitation to connect, and another suggested podcast episode.

Email 4 contains three tips for the about page with a messaging clarity worksheet.

Email 5 is the services page with my ultra-clear tagline formula, a link to my workbooks, and another podcast episode.

Email 6 is a sneak preview of a new offer I'm excited to share, usually a workbook or workshop.

The purpose of each of these emails is:
1. To introduce them to me, my point of view, and my offers
2. To be of service with useful, interesting information
3. To provide a few cozy minutes, a moment of sweetness, a surprise present

While it's not a hard rule, I recommend focusing on delivering value instead of going for the sale in these introductory emails because the main job is to build a long-term relationship. But sometimes paying you is the next logical step—and one they're ready to take. If that's the case, go for it.

The most common pitfall I see in freebies: Thinly-veiled sales pitches posing as webinars, workshops, and "free" classes

I once spent 37 minutes on a webinar—given by a well-known, reputable copywriter—waiting for the promised value: a short stack of copywriting formulas. Instead, I got her life story and a sales pitch for her upcoming program. Finally, at minute 37.6, she gave up the goods…and they weren't that good. Then, for the next 20 minutes, it was back to the sales pitch. *I was livid.*

As a consumer, you've likely been through the free webinar, workshop, or class that promises valuable information and does not deliver. In fact, by now you've been *trained* to expect a sales pitch. So when you show up, you're not really paying attention (why would you?). You're turning off your camera, checking your emails, filing your nails, going to the bathroom…

How effectively do you think that webinar will sell under those conditions?

It's not effective. Not at all.

But wait! It got people's email addresses, right? It worked at least to *build the list!*

Let's say you got 50 people's email addresses. Twenty of them show up to the webinar to be underwhelmed and another five skim through the recording, hunting for the promised information in the haystack of the sales pitch. The other 25 forget about you entirely until you pop up in their inbox, where they (at best) unsubscribe or worse, mark you as spam or ignore you completely (ruining your open rates and damaging your credibility as an email contact so your future communications are automatically filtered into the spam folder). Eventually, you have a large list of completely disengaged readers. Services like Mailchimp charge based on list size, not open rates, so you're wasting your time AND money.

I've seen this chain reaction happen to good business owners repeatedly because someone told them, "Webinars are the way!" But then told them to sell rather than deliver value.

When I develop webinar scripts with my clients, I spend the first minute of the script setting expectations:

> "Welcome! I'm so glad you're here. First, let me say this will not be an extended sales pitch for my program. I will spend the last 10 minutes talking about my program and answering questions, but for the next 50 minutes, it's ALL value, and you will be able to do [tangible, actionable thing] by the end. So pay attention and get ready to take notes because we'll cover a lot of info fast."

If I include a sales pitch, not only do I place it at the end of the workshop—after I've delivered real value—I tell them up front that's what I'm doing. So they pay attention on the call. So the ones watching the recording don't try to skim to where they assume the real value is. So they know this webinar is *different*.

This is one place you can start to train people to expect to get value from you.

Full disclosure: I was raised by a horse trainer, my mother-in-law is a dog trainer, and I spend a long weekend every year learning how to train camels (you read that right), so I think in terms of animal behavior. And let me tell you: You can't get a 2,000-pound camel to do anything it doesn't want to do. They're incredibly smart animals, so they remember if you promise them a grain cookie and don't deliver. Good luck getting them to do ANYTHING next time!

Humans and camels have a lot more in common than you might think. So you want to train them with cookies (value), and when they take an action that you ask them to do, you deliver the cookie. Every. Time.[39]

---

[39] Public service announcement: Don't be *that* person trying to get a selfie with a camel by holding the cookie just outside the camel's reach until you get the photo. It annoys the camel and trains them to bite you, because if they bite you, they get the cookie really fast. Please apply this principle to humans as well. Do not withhold the cookie!

Your freebie is one of the first touchpoints prospective clients have with you, which makes it a vitally important tool for building a relationship based on trust and the expectation of positive outcomes. Deliver value here, and continue to deliver value with every email, and you will have a growing list of engaged prospective clients.

How to know if your freebie is working

With consent-based list building, your list will grow more slowly, which makes numbers a less important metric of freebie success. Because you're not only after subscribers, your goal is to have engaged subscribers. Here are a few success indicators worth tracking:
- Number of subscribers who come through your ungated freebie. This number indicates the accessibility and value of your freebie. Once you have a baseline number of subscribers/month, you can tweak the freebie itself to make it even more valuable or alter the newsletter CTA copy to increase subscriptions.
- Social media shares, if that applies. Or number of downloads.
- Subscriber engagement with newsletters and sales emails (more on that in the next chapter).
    - Keep a log of how many replies you get when you send out a newsletter. My subscribers often hit reply like they're talking to a friend because they are!
    - Check your open rates. When you've trained your subscribers to expect value, your open rates will be higher (often much higher) than your industry average.
    - How long it takes you to fill up a course, program,

or workshop. The healthier your list, the more likely they are to buy from you (and buy quickly).

Remember:

 *Setting expectations for your entire working relationship often starts with your freebie. Always deliver the cookie when you offer a webinar, a gift session, a limited-series podcast, a PDF, or anything else.*

But let's be honest: The world doesn't need more freebies. It needs more generously useful, trust-building resources. Be the one who surprises your audience with real value and they'll stick around long after the cookie crumbs are gone.

Takeaways

1. **Make freebies actually free:** If you're offering a "freebie," remove the gatekeeping. Deliver your content without requiring an email address or personal information, then invite people to deepen the relationship by joining your email list—enthusiastically and by choice. You can also lead with a simple invitation to your newsletter, with an introductory email series that delivers value and delight.
2. **Deliver real value:** Avoid fluff. Design your freebie to offer tangible, actionable, and immediate benefits. Let it provide a clear taste of what it's like to work with you while solving a small but meaningful problem for your audience.
3. **Be transparent about sales:** If a webinar or freebie includes a sales pitch, say so in the first minute, tell them it's at the end, and keep the pitch portion short. The rest of the webinar or workshop should deliver on your promises with enough value to satisfy people regardless of whether they buy.
4. **Engage with generosity:** Surprise and delight your audience by exceeding their expectations. Generous freebies and welcome email sequences build trust and inspire word-of-mouth referrals and positive associations with your brand.
5. **Train your audience with value:** Set a precedent of reliability and respect by consistently delivering what you promise. *Give them the cookie every time. Do not withhold the cookie!* (And by cookie, I mean actionable takeaways and positive emotions.) This builds trust and ensures your audience returns eager for more rather than feeling manipulated, cheated, or disappointed.

CHAPTER 8

Emails That Get Read (and Not Because of Clickbait Titles)

Now that you're building your list with enthusiastic consent, you're ready to create some ultra-engaging newsletters!

Often, as business owners, we assume that we should write newsletters because that's what business owners do. If you're fortunate enough to have a business coach, they will likely tell you to "get cracking with the content!" But before you do, stop to wonder if a newsletter is how you enjoy connecting with your ideal clients because, while it's a good way, it's not the only way. If you dislike writing, try making videos on YouTube or sending them to your list via email. If you shudder at having your face visible on video, take a video of your hands knitting or painting or flipping tarot cards while you speak or record a subscriber-only podcast. The limit is your imagination and what your clients enjoy receiving.

If you're still sold on newsletters, I want you to explore your motivation (and it has to be better than "my business coach told me to" or you'll never stick with it).

In my workshop "Newsletters That Get Read: for Small Businesses with Small Lists," my first question is, "Why are you doing this anyway?!"

Because not long ago, I was very resistant to starting a newsletter. As a professional copywriter who writes for hours every day, asking me to add one more writing assignment to my week got a big HELL NO for years. Confession: I'm a writer who doesn't love writing. I'd rather be doing one hundred other things. I only journal under extreme duress, didn't keep a diary as a kid for longer than a week, and don't dream of becoming a novelist (even though I have a dozen ideas for murder mysteries with toxic botanicals as murder weapons).

Many of my clients also resist spending time on what is, for them, a chore.

You'll often hear this practical reason to write a newsletter as a primary form of marketing: You own your list in a way you will never own your social media accounts. It can't be taken away from you, and you can't be locked out (unless you forget your password).

But the more profound reason is this: The people willing to lay their inboxes on the line for you are your people. They are the ones who are invested in your success, want to hear what you have to say, and will support you in ways no casual social media follower will.

Based on surveys of nearly 10,400 consumers worldwide in late 2023…
- 50% had made purchases from emails in the previous year (compared with 43% from social media posts)
- 63% said they pay more to shop with brands they're loyal to
- 85% said their favorite brand "treats them like an individual"[40]

Your subscribers allow you in their inboxes because they trust you, and they trust you because you treat them with respect.

Your subscribers are not only more likely to buy from you repeatedly,

---

[40] "2024 Global Consumer Trends Index," *Marigold, with EConsultancy*, January 2024.

they're also more likely to refer you to their friends (and referred people refer more people).[41] They may even *become* your friends.

Newsletters (and email marketing in general) can help you form the closer relationships that create sustainable businesses. Email is not the only way, but it's a great way. And it feels terrific when your readers "hit reply" like you just sent them a personal letter…because, in a way, you did.

Now let's look at the other side of the equation: Why do your clients sign up to receive newsletters? Especially now, when every business has a newsletter and our inboxes are constantly bombarded with ads, emails, and more content than we can possibly consume. Why on earth would anyone sign up for one more goddamn email?

Confession time: The hardest part of being an entrepreneur, for me, is staying on top of my inbox. So this is a sore spot. And yet, I also, often, sign up for newsletters.

Newsletters are a way to stay connected with people we care about, are curious about, or would like to get to know more. Sometimes, they're peaceful moments of our day. Sometimes, they contain an interesting story, or a cute animal photo, or other delightful surprise. And, sometimes, they introduce ways to work with people we know, like, and trust.

But there are other reasons to sign up for newsletters that aren't so wholesome and that some business owners leverage.
- The promise of transformation: Content that capitalizes on transformation lures readers in with grand promises and "imagine if" scenarios but doesn't deliver any actual

---

[41] Referred customers not only buy more, they also refer 30 to 57% more new customers than people who found a business without a referral. Gershon, R., & Jiang, Z. (2025). Referral Contagion: Downstream Benefits of Customer Referrals. Journal of Marketing Research, 62(1), 97-116. https://doi.org/10.1177/00222437241257886

help unless you pay for the privilege.
- A salve to loneliness: So many people crave feeling seen and understood by someone who truly gets them. This becomes dangerous when you position yourself as more of a friend and confidant than you are prepared to be or could possibly be. One business growth program promises "the friendship and unconditional love you've been looking for your whole life."42 Be wary of seducing and charming your way into people's pockets by overpromising emotional connection.
- FOMO (fear of missing out) on something valuable or entertaining: For a newsletter subscription, I'm not nearly as concerned about FOMO as, say, using it to pressure someone into spending hundreds or thousands on your program. But if you're using FOMO to get people to subscribe to your newsletter with promises like "subscribe to receive special deals and discounts, with limited time bonus access to subscriber-only offers," then you might get a few more subscribers, but are they there for the right reasons? Or are they just trying to get a deal? In my experience, prospects who try to get a bargain are miserable to work with as clients.

In this chapter, I am going to teach you how to write delightful, charming, engaging, friendly newsletters that build relationships. But as you work to connect with your audience, make sure you're lifting them up rather than using their insecurities to boost your open rates.

---

42 Boldheart Business Program sales page, boldheart.com/programs, as of January 5, 2025.

How to invite subscribers (for the right reasons)

Your ideal client's experience with your newsletter starts with the invitation, usually as a section on your home page or in the footer (at the bottom of every page). It typically has an area for their name and email address only.

If you leave it at "Sign up for my newsletter," nobody will join your newsletter unless you already have a relationship. Your readership will be limited to your mother and your best friend from sixth grade. Your mother will helpfully email you back every time she spots a typo.

When you're ready to expand your readership past your built-in superfans *and* you're not luring in unsuspecting people who just want your "freebie," you must make the invitation clear and appealing. Some treat it like a short sales pitch: Tell them what they're getting and why they want it. Tell them the problems your newsletter helps solve.

That is an acceptable approach. But it sets up a transactional relationship when most service-based business owners I work with want something warmer and more personal to build longer-term relationships.

Here's how Susannah Conway, one of the best newsletter writers out there, invited her readers to her list:

Let me send you letters…

Twice a month I send out Love Letters. They're not "newsletters" because, quite frankly, newsletters are boring. No, I send out missives written from my heart about what's really going on—in my life, in my work, stuff I'm healing, epiphanies I've had. The letters are the running story of what it takes to live a heart-centred creative life as a woman in this world. They are about my life, but I hope you see a bit of you reflected back, too. The Love Letters are my lighthouse, the place I shine my light so we ALL find our way to shore (and avoid the rocks!).

When you sign up to the Love Letters you also get access to The Library, a secret page filled with ebooks to inspire you, meditations to ground and centre you, and desktop wallpapers that turn your computer into a contemplative space. Alongside the rambles, I'll share updates on anything worth knowing including my free community projects and course discount codes. If you're curious, you can read a recent Love Letter <u>over here</u>.

Sign up for love

<u>Email address</u> →

Susannah's invitation is long and her newsletters are also long, so even the invitation sets up an accurate expectation of what you'll get. But, structurally, this invitation has everything you need, even if you write your version more concisely.

1. It begins with setting expectations of how often you'll see her in your inbox.
2. It tells you what her letters will be about.
3. She conveys what it will *feel like* to read her letters—the emotional promise that underpins her entire brand. To paraphrase Maya Angelou, people will forget what you say but won't forget how you make them feel. This is 100% true for newsletters. Use responsibly.
4. *Then,* Susannah offers a free thing—but what you're signing up for, primarily, is the newsletter itself. The

newsletter has intrinsic value. And, generously, she's also offering access to a useful resource.

5. Finally, her call-to-action language is "Sign Up for love." I like how she is invoking the central promise again of what it feels like to receive a letter from her. I also know (because I read all of her newsletters) that she delivers on that promise. However, I might raise an eyebrow if another business owner did this. Should you be promising to make someone feel loved? Is that preying upon someone's desperate need to feel loved? Or is it purely supportive and, well, *loving*? I don't have an answer for you.

I can tell you that her newsletter list is vast, and, as one of its many members, I feel the love come through—and that's what keeps me coming back. Plus, she includes baby fox and kitten photos in her emails. The open-rate value of regularly including adorable animal photos in your newsletter cannot be overstated, and she had a whole season of taking photos of baby foxes in her backyard.

The final piece of the invitation that many people leave out is a testimonial just for your newsletter. Ask your readers to tell you why they like your newsletter and choose a testimonial that speaks to the emotional experience (or other primary value) of receiving it. Here is the testimonial under Susannah Conway's newsletter invitation:

It feels like a letter from a friend

"They're just honest. It feels like a letter from a friend. They're not overly salesy or even "valuable" and I don't mean that in a bad way, I just mean you're not constantly trying ot shove

VALUE down our throughts. Its nice to just read sweet stories and vulnerable explorations. And yes, sometimes I learn things or am inspired by something you've created, but mostly your emails are just enjoyable to read."

MARIAN | GERMANY

I love that this testimonial proves you don't constantly have to "shove VALUE" at your readers. You are inherently valuable. Your thoughts, ideas, opinions, and observations are enough. If you want to add more value to that, great. If not, you don't have to. In the words of author E.M. Forster, "Only connect."

Before you sit down to write, ask yourself: Am I inviting connection only to make you like me and buy my stuff? Or am I inviting connection because it's mutually rewarding, I genuinely enjoy your company, and if it's a fit, I can offer something you need in return for what I need (e.g., to pay my bills)?

The action—in this case, the newsletter—is the same, but the motivation is different. I believe motivation matters.

If the energy you bring to your newsletter is transactional and extractive, that is the kind of relationship you will cultivate. If the energy you bring is reciprocal and regenerative, those relationships will sustain your business and feed your soul.

The automated welcome email

Once you've invited your readers to your inbox party, there's one more thing I like to do before they start receiving my irregular newsletters:[43] Before I created my current six-email Starter Kit sequence, I had just one automated "welcome to my newsletter" email that automatically sent as soon as new readers signed up. This is still the first email new readers receive, even though now it's followed by a crash course in ethical copywriting.

In this welcome letter, I introduce myself, tell a little bit of my entrepreneurial origin story, and state my values. I also include an indigenous land acknowledgement and a diversity and inclusion statement to make sure everyone feels welcome. Then I tell my readers what to expect that they'll enjoy (reinforcing the promises made in the invitation that this is "a downright delightful letter"). Finally, I invite them to hit reply any time because I read all of the replies (they give me life, even when my inbox is a hot mess). I let them know they can unsubscribe if it gets to be too much—no hard feelings.

When this was a stand-alone welcome email, I also included *a lil treat*: just a fun free thing that tickled my fancy (now there's a big treat with every email in the sequence!). If you sign up for newsletters from copywriters who specialize in email marketing, you'll notice: They. All. Give. Treats. It's like Halloween night on Main Street America around here, and they're handing out the full-sized candy bars.

My first (automated) email sets the tone for all following communications. It also has an impressive open rate of 79% because the people who sign up for my newsletters are genuinely interested in receiving them (the benefit of not tricking them into it!).

---

[43] I'm terrible with consistency. The good news is: Contrary to popular advice, it is possible to build a highly engaged list without writing consistently.

You can send one or several automated emails in a welcome series to train your readers to open everything you send in the future. And yes, each of these should contain a treat. It's a good strategy if you don't send too many emails too often (which will train your readers to ignore you or mark your emails as spam).

How to ruin your open rates and what to do if you already have

Many clients come to me after accidentally training their readers NOT to open their emails. So let me explain how open rates get ruined:

- Your list is artificially inflated (you made a quiz, didn't you?).
- Your emails are always selling a product/service.
- You only talk about what you do and why they should buy (all business, no pleasure).
- You're 100% instructive/educational (boring!).
- You send emails too often, all the time (not just picking up the pace when you're launching).
- You use a script or template that was handed to you by a well-meaning coach or program that sounds more like them than you.
- You feed your people through a multi-email funnel that starts with a bad freebie and ends with a blast of sales emails they're not ready for and never consented to.

If your open rates are abysmal and you've engaged in any of the above practices (or all of them), all is not lost. Yes, you've biffed it. But you can relaunch your newsletter to your list. Send an email apologizing for spamming them and announcing your fresh intention. Offer them something fun and free as a sign of goodwill. Then, tell them what they can expect from you in the future. Finally, invite them to unsubscribe if what you'll be sending isn't a good fit.

You will probably get a bunch of unsubscribes, but that is what you're going for. The ones who stay are your true readers.

Five steps to rebuild trust with your readers:
1. Start with a heartfelt apology and express gratitude that they're still here.
2. Outline your new approach and what benefits they can expect if they stay.
3. Include a short, engaging, personal story to reestablish the relationship (you may want to lead with this and bridge into the apology).
4. Share an exciting preview of the content they'll receive.
5. Give a fun gift as a goodwill gesture.

This method also works if you are changing your niche or entire business, and you want to see if any members of your current list are interested in following you on your next adventure. Just switch the apology with an explanation.

Writing your newsletter

Finally, you're ready to write the actual newsletter itself. First, let me ask you this: What do the newsletters that survive the trash and spam folders of your inbox have in common?

I've identified four must-haves:
1. They're personal—not just "all business" and certainly

not all sales.
2. They're entertaining—they have to be intrinsically rewarding to read.
3. They're informative—there has to be value in there, too.
4. They contain a treat (see cookies and camels in Chapter 7).

They are also usually fun, relatable, and validating.

You don't need all these elements in every newsletter, but you need at least two in any combination. Why? Because you are training your readers to open your newsletters.

Here's the ethically gray area: Is it manipulative to give someone a treat every time they complete a desired action? Treat theory activates the same dopamine cocktail that makes social media so addictive. Clearly, knowing how to make someone feel good can be used for evil. The question is: Can you use it for good? For me, the answer is yes.

My background is in training large animals (and small animals, who, oddly, are harder—ever try to house-train a chihuahua?). So this is where I stand: As long as everybody wins and nobody is shamed or punished if they don't comply, it's fine. If you're not even comfortable training your dog to sit, this might make you feel uncomfortable. Because what I'm talking about is positive reinforcement training: Rewarding desired behaviors every time they happen.

Or what I like to call Treat Theory.

Animals and people will do pretty much anything for a treat. For camels, it's grain cookies and apples. For humans, it's personal connection, entertainment, and curiosity/interests/surprises.

When you send your welcome email or welcome sequence, include "high-value" treats, like an extremely useful template or access to a limited series podcast. Email copywriter Tarzan Kay's welcome series is about how to write a welcome series—it's brilliant.

In your regular newsletter, you don't need to hand out the

grain cookies—sorry, that's for camels—you can switch it out with apples—camels again! Sorry! What I mean is: You don't need to give high-value treats all the time. But don't enter someone's inbox empty handed. I include a "Free Fun Thing" section in every newsletter that contains either something free I'm offering or something free one of my clients is offering. And if I don't currently have something to promote, I end every newsletter with the current book I'm reading and the podcast I'm listening to (I also used to share what tea I was drinking, but after four years, I ran out of ideas).

When it's time to launch a paid course or larger-scale offer, however, that's when the high-value treats come back out. To paraphrase my longtime business coach, Caroline Leon, launches are when you shower your subscribers with gifts. This makes sense because launches, when you send out many more emails than usual and they're all selling something, are when you get the most unsubscribes. Treats incentivize your readers to stay, even if they're not interested in the offer you're currently launching.

Treat Theory isn't just for your readers. It also applies to us, the content creators. I resisted writing newsletters for my business for years, thinking, "Dear heaven, you want me to write one more thing?! I write all day!" I was like the professional chef who won't cook at home. Part of it was overwhelm and part of it was believing that my newsletter had to contain "news" or something "useful." I didn't have news and wasn't interested in talking shop about copywriting. What was left? My answer came back around to connection.

It almost doesn't matter what you write about as long as you connect with love and humor. Share your enthusiasm. Invite people to your party and have great conversations. Be vulnerable when you struggle. When I figured THAT out, I got hooked on writing newsletters. They weren't just about building a list—they became a way to invite the humans on the other side of the screen to play.

With every newsletter you send, *you* get a little treat.

Newsletter structure

Every email you love has the same structure. Yes, really. Once you see it, you'll never unsee it.

> Subject line: Contains a benefit, emotion, action, curious statement, or urgency
>
> Part 1: Anecdote that may, or may not, have anything to do with what you do for work, but you will tie it into a teachable moment that connects with your work anyway
>
> Part 2: Short bridge between anecdote, the teachable moment or idea it sparked, and what you do or sell
>
> Part 3: Your current offer or a fun free thing (a lil treat!) with a call-to-action
>
> Part 4: Connection points—an interesting article you just read, your favorite cheap-but-flattering top you found on Amazon, your latest podcast listen
>
> Part 5: Signature (something catchy)

This structure is simple, fun, effective, and a potential minefield of questionable practices. For example, you could use a clickbait subject line like "You won't believe what's inside this email!" or "Top secret strategies for guaranteed success!" eroding your credibility. Or you can leverage FOMO like, "Uh-oh, you're missing out on the best deal of the year" or "Your seven-figure plan goes bye-bye at midnight." You can overpromise with a credulity-stretching result like, "10X your email list in three days!" (that you cannot possibly guarantee). You can play into their fears about their body/age/hair. All of these will get you clicks…once.

Fool me once, shame on you. Fool me twice, you get labeled as SPAM.

My subject lines tend to be funny and honest but not too flashy. I don't have to worry about making them "clickable" since I've already trained my readers to expect a positive experience with every email. I always include an interesting story, a lil treat, and ideas for what to read and listen to.

The moral is: Don't get too clever with your subject lines. Focus more on the quality of the content inside your email. This advice runs contrary to almost everything you'll read about email marketing (but so much of that advice is for product-based businesses; service-based business owners are playing a completely different game—a game won with relationships, not gimmicks).

How to find the right story to tell

The gold your readers will come back for is the story: the funny, endearing, vulnerable, personal anecdote that starts the newsletter. I am often asked, "How do you know what to write about?" And my answer is: free association.[44] Messaging expert Rachael Cumberland-Dodd started one of her emails with a story about boxing:

---

[44] Psychology. Noun. The mental process by which one word or image may spontaneously suggest another without any apparent connection. Definition from Oxford Languages.

I've been hanging out in a boxing gym of late.
One of those old-skool sweat and sawdust gyms—where the tangy smell of Lynx Africa blends with the whiff of musty jockstraps and the pong of dried blood.

Mmmm. I love it!

Boxing, I've discovered = the best fricking exercise; always on the balls on your feet, brain dancing as your sparring partner barks 'jab, jab, hook' through his mustache.

Jab jab hook
Connect, oof, thwack
And lo, as I was prancing around the ring last week, a weirdo thought popped into my head.

Huh, Boxing and Marketing, they're all about the connection equation.
Glove meets pad
Need meets solution
Fist meets punchbag
Empathy meets action

So armed with this revelation, I have figured out what the Jab, Jab, Hook of your marketing is....
Three little words (or two if you don't want to swear) that you should utter every time you sit down to write.

Jab, jab, hook = **So fecking What.**

So What is a neat little hack that instantly shifts the focus from:
'What do I want to say' to
'What do they need to hear?

The key to successful free association is to have a pad of paper and a pen handy when your mind wanders and starts to make connections between that grilled cheese sandwich you're eating and how you guide people through somatically processing their early childhood trauma. It takes practice to catch inspiration when it lands.

If you're reading Rachael's boxing story and thinking, "I could never come up with that" or "I could never write a story in such a fun way," you are not alone. I couldn't either. Which brings me to my next point: writing style.

What's your writing style?

"Write how you speak" isn't actionable advice for everyone, especially if you've been trained by academia, government, or another institution to write formally. But even in the most formal settings, you can include:

- Personal stories to build connection—tiny events that happened throughout your day, like the conversation you had with the barista when ordering coffee (think snapshots, not The Hero's Journey)
- Humor to get your reader to pay attention
- Self-deprecation to come across as human and relatable

If you're stuck on how to write with your authentic voice, relax. You probably already are. If you can shed the "shoulds" you've absorbed from other people (high school English teachers tend to be the worst culprits, unless you went into higher academia or, *heaven forbid,* a creative writing class) and say what you really think, that's ninety percent of the battle. The other ten percent is basic grammar and spelling. I've worked with so many talented entrepreneurs who've been told they're bad at writing, and they are not. Neither are you. It's not about finding your authentic voice. It's about finding the confidence to use it.

That said, possibly the most important key to improving your writing style is: Write for a single reader.

Copywriters are trained to write for "one reader," or what you may have heard called the "ideal client avatar." But the essential concept is to write like you're speaking to just one person. That one person happens to be your ideal client. Yes, you are blasting your newsletter out to hundreds of subscribers, but you will have an easier time writing it, and you'll write it more effectively, if you write with one person in mind. You can also give yourself permission to shake off formality and have some fun because your one reader—your ideal client—won't think less of you for it. They'll like you even more.

The selling part (don't panic)

After your story, you'll likely want to connect it with an offer or a free thing. This is where many of my clients run into trouble because it can feel awkward! One moment, you're telling a cozy story about taking your dog for a walk in the woods, and the next minute, you're selling your mastermind program. Suddenly, the genuine connection you've been mindfully building feels like a lure to a sales call.

Icky!

Let's look at what's going on here because it's rarely as icky as it feels to you.

Your readers know that you run a business and that, sometimes, you will include ways to work with you or offers that might benefit them. In sharing your offers, you are, in fact, being of service. After all, they are on your list because A) they like you and B) they're considering buying from you.

Yes, you write your newsletter like a letter to a friend—and it is—but newsletters are also marketing, and your readers understand that. It's great to offer them a story. It's wonderful to share a lesson you've learned that might benefit them. And it is absolutely fine to mention the offer you're currently promoting. You don't even need to transition into it. Just give your offer its own regular section so your readers know where to find it.

The final part of the email is my favorite: connection points. This is where I get to be an "influencer" and give some love to my favorite authors, podcasters, and indie tea companies. I also frequently highlight previous clients' offers in my newsletter to help expand their reach. I go into full Oprah mode during the holidays and send a "Lauren's Favorite Things" email.

You can have fun with your newsletter! Your newsletter can highlight other businesses, service providers, and products you love. You can use it as your soapbox, pulpit, or podium to share your philosophy.

You can use your newsletter to build community.

When you are brainstorming newsletter content, consider:
- What information or insights can you offer that might be of use?
- How would you like your readers to feel?

- How can you add delight, entertainment, humor, and fun to your emails?
- In what ways can you be generous with your readers?
- What do your readers need in terms of accessibility?

One of my past clients thought deeply about what her people needed, which changed her approach to writing newsletters. Her readers were new mothers who were exhausted and had no time to read a lengthy email, so she made her newsletters three- to five-minute reads that contained a single, practical, instantly implementable tip. Perfect for checking emails in the bathroom while your toddler is pounding at the door.

Five things I wish every service-based business owner knew about their newsletter:

1. Your newsletter is not your blog, diary, or autobiography, and it's not the place to process your complex trauma. It is the place to come after you've figured something out and want to share it with people. You can let them in on the process of figuring something out, too. You don't always need to have the answers, but remember that the newsletter should be of service to your readers and isn't your personal processing space.
2. TL;DR: Too long; didn't read is a real problem. I love starting my newsletters with a personal story (I think everyone should because it's fun, engaging, and builds real relationships!). I'm also aware of not asking for too much of my readers' time and attention spans. Writing long is often just self-indulgent (though there are notable

exceptions,[45] and maybe you're one of them).
3. *Too much news, not enough letter* is boring and won't produce higher open rates or reader engagement. Make it personal.
4. Don't try to cram material for five newsletters into one—i.e., flitting from topic to topic instead of choosing one to dive deeply into.
5. Consistency and frequency are overrated. Everyone tells you "be consistent with your content" or "write a newsletter every week." But, in my personal experience, weekly newsletters are a lot (both to write and to receive) and I don't read half of the ones I get. I send a newsletter once a month when I feel like it, and because my readers know the newsletters are fun, my open rates and engagement (aka replies) are high. If consistency and high frequency work for you and you enjoy it, please continue. But if that "should" creates too much pressure and overwhelm, then you have my permission to write monthly or at any pace that works for you and your readers.

---

[45] Notable exceptions: Tad Hargrave of Marketing for Hippies, Susannah Conway, Sharon Blackie, and Andréa Jones of OnlineDrea. They all write long, and I read every word.

Takeaways

1. **Support agency, autonomy, and choice:** Don't automatically dump people into your email list when they sign up for "freebies," webinars, and quizzes.
2. **Invite instead:** Invite people to join your list after they've found value in your actually-free freebie, webinar, or quiz. You can also just invite people to subscribe to your newsletter based on its own merits.
3. **Sell it:** When writing CTA copy for your newsletter, include the following information:
   d. How often you send it
   e. What the newsletter is about
   f. How your readers will benefit from reading it
   g. Why they want it
4. **Express gratitude graciously:** In your "thank you for subscribing" email, introduce yourself and welcome your new readers with a lil treat.
5. **"No thanks" is always okay:** Give readers the option to unsubscribe in every email.
6. **Automated welcome email outline**
   Subject: You're in…for a treat (welcome!)
   Part 1: I'm so glad you're here. This is what you can expect.
   Part 2: TREAT! Give them something fun.
   Part 3: Introduce yourself to anyone meeting you for the first time. Include your name, what you do, who you do it for, and what problems you help solve for them.
   Part 4: Who ARE you to be an authority on your topic? What is your experience or expertise?
   Part 5: Values statement.
   Part 6: Outline what your newsletters will include

(remember treats).

Part 7: Invite them to hit reply and give them the option to unsubscribe.

Part 8: Email signature—it doesn't need to be fancy; it can just be your name. But you might also include a catchphrase. Mine is: *Make every word a force for good.*

CHAPTER 9

Social Media Done Dirty

I've curated my Instagram feed to manipulate me on purpose. This began when I went all-in on intuitive eating and health at every size (HAES) but was still having terrible body image days. One afternoon I was walking home from Pilates in tears because I will never be thin in a society hostile to fat people. Then I scrolled through Instagram and saw a post from Jameela Jamil, actress and activist who uses her Instagram account to criticize diet culture and advocate for body neutrality. Seeing her post about the health issues she's suffered from calorie restriction, ending with the reminder that thinness doesn't equal happiness, reconnected me with my values as if I'd had a conversation with a friend. I felt better. I smiled.

And then I ruthlessly curated my feed. I added mid-size and plus-size fashion influencers and deleted straight-size ones. I only followed fitness influencers in larger bodies. I started following psychologists and nutritionists who were passionate about intuitive eating. I removed all content about weight loss and restrictive eating. In just a few weeks, I noticed that when I looked in the mirror in the morning, I felt good about myself. I observed my internalized fatphobia shrink (the only part of myself I want to shrink!) and my perception of what I found beautiful expanded. I used the manipulative power of social media to reprogram my brain in a positive way, but I could only do so because business owners (and a precious few celebrities) use that platform to inform, inspire, and spread their counter-diet-culture point of view.

There's been a growing trend to leave social media among conscious entrepreneurs who are rightly sick of the companies that own these platforms and the small-minded people endlessly arguing on them. If you are exhausted by social media, I would urge you to first curate your feed (ruthlessly), and if you still feel the same, find another way to connect with your people. There are plenty of ways out there.[46]

But if you are willing to stick it out with these platforms, keep the potential for good in mind. Your content can be a turning point in someone's day or someone's life. You can lift someone up who you've never met and introduce them to ideas they've never considered (or remind them of the values they hold dear). Dare I say, you can use social media to empower.[47] Even with the constant algorithm changes, these channels are still an excellent way to reach people, connect with clients, and build relationships. The key is to avoid being sucked into the manipulative and outright dishonest practices *we almost don't notice* because they're everywhere.

This chapter is going to be tightly focused on the ethical aspects of social media content and how you can use these platforms for good. But I am not a social media strategist—I just write the words. If you're looking for social media strategy, see the Resources section in the back of the book.

---

[46] Anti-capitalist business strategist Maggie Gentry hasn't been on social media since September 2020. She uses her marketing time to pitch podcasts instead. There are so many options!

[47] As a copywriter, I try to avoid the word "empower" because it is *so* overused. Pro tip: Don't use it in your copy, even if it's exactly what you do. Instead, describe what it means to empower your clients and what empowerment looks like in their everyday lives.

Don't like it? Use it

I have a confession: While I curate my feed mercilessly and keep (almost) only what brings me joy and much-needed perspective…I do follow a few people in my industry specifically because I am enraged by their marketing. I don't comment on their content or troll them, but I do use their posts as fuel for my content ideas: Everything I'd like to yell at them becomes a point-of-view-packed post for my audience. I just have to be careful to balance righteous rage with inspiration and coziness because my brand is more about the cozy. I figure people need a respite from the righteous rage already online.

When you see a post or another business account that makes your skin crawl and your pulse quicken, take notice. They're doing something that contradicts your values. When you take a moment to trace the outrage-to-values connection, it can be the first step to dreaming up content that does the opposite and sets your business apart.

I have a method for making sure my rage-inspired posts don't get too snarky or angry (which is not my brand vibe and not one I wish to cultivate). I write two drafts. The first one is my hot take, and it is *ghost-pepper-hot*. Then I give myself time to cool down and revise it. I ask: What about this will serve my audience best?

The problematic lifestyle promise

One type of social media post that is guaranteed to grind my gears is the "my life is amazing and yours can be, too…when you buy my program!" Here's why this common trope is a big problem.

Picture this: A conventionally beautiful woman with long wavy hair and a trendy outfit walks away from the camera toward a colorful European city—Spain? Italy? South of France? Who knows? The caption reads: "What if you were eight weeks away from..."

Then she sells her eight-week program, which is not about traveling. It is very much about creating an online business with the implicit promise that, in two months, you'll be making enough income to stroll the streets of Venice.

Picture this: She's on a beach now, with clear blue Mediterranean water and a resort in the background, holding a glass of Prosecco toward the camera as the sun sets. The caption: "If one of your dreams is to *finally* start a creative side hustle from home..."

Now she's sipping an Aperol spritz (is that another charming Italian town in the background?), and the caption reads, "I think I can make your life so much easier and so much cooler if I taught you how to get PAID to work from anywhere."

It's seductive. The implicit promise in these "lifestyle photos" is if you buy my program, you'll make enough money to travel like a Hollywood A-lister and that this is an achievable result for anyone, with no mention of outside factors. Never mind if the business owner is married to an investment banker, has inherited wealth, or maybe just has a friend with a boat. You don't get that level of insider information, because they're selling a dream, not the reality, and certainly not the actual results their typical clients have gained from their program. There is no guarantee of results and no mention of the number of program graduates who earn a high income or how long it takes them to make a living wage. And privilege is almost never mentioned because you can't "imagine if" someone into magically becoming a conventionally attractive middle-class white woman when they buy your program.

Often, these business owners are not even sharing their real numbers. Listen, I am all for sharing your vacay photos—I can't wait to see them. But don't use them to promise your audience they can do it, too…unless you're a travel agent.

Social media marketing is at its most manipulative when it sets up unreasonable, impossible expectations in order to sell a product or service. Here, we run into the same ethical problems we ran into in Chapter 6 when you write your about page as your "success story:" lack of transparency about what it really takes to get results and transparency around the results themselves.

But my favorite posts are the ones by influencers who show the real story, like the fitness influencer who posted an entire mock "weight loss montage" that looked like it took six months, but that she recorded in one hour (by puffing out her belly in the beginning, changing clothes five times, and sucking in her belly for the "after" photo at the end). I also love the fitness influencers who show belly profiles before they eat breakfast (hello, abs!) and after they eat breakfast, lunch, and dinner. (Surprise! Their bodies expand and contract just like everyone else's!) These business owners are using the tropes of their industry to create content that helps their audiences feel more confident, not less. Their follower counts soar. Their viewers share their posts. And their businesses make a positive impact in the world while making money.

It can be done.

Finding the right balance

I am not a social media strategist, and it shows. But I have learned to balance my content with informative posts, personal posts, and advertising posts. With each type of post, I think:
- What information would help my ideal clients today?

- What would delight my ideal clients when they scroll through their feed?
- What are other businesses in my niche doing that I don't like and what can I do differently?
- How can I infuse my content with my unique point of view?
- How can I meaningfully, and personally, connect with my people?

The posts that come out of that thought process are informative and often take a contrarian perspective on mainstream marketing and copywriting tactics. They contain strong opinions, generous tips, and occasional craft, cat, and chicken photos. When I publish personal posts with my face (for higher engagement), I never use a filter, half the time I'm not wearing makeup, and my hair is far from salon-perfect—mostly because if I waited for all of those stars to align, I'd never show up at all.

I think that's the key to social media. Showing up imperfectly, authentically, and consistently. You don't have to figure out the latest gimmick or algorithm hack if that fries your brain. Your people will still find you because they want reminders that you exist, they want your unique energy in their orbit, they want content that they can use and share, and eventually, they want to buy. Give them content that supports those goals.

Seven principles of ethical social media content

So how can you, as an ethical business owner, create content to expand your reach and sell your offers through social media?

1. Choose one platform to "major in" and get really good at it. Instagram is my favorite, but if you're comfortable

on Facebook, do that. If you gravitate toward TikTok, play there. If you love writing, Substack is having a major moment. If you're already on one of the newer platforms (I can never keep track), take advantage of the clear playing field to own your niche. The "best" platform is the one you'll actually use. *This isn't an ethical point, just a practical one.*

2. Preach! One of my favorite business and marketing coaches often speaks of using his social media presence like a pulpit to preach his philosophy. I love that. Use your platform to dive deep into what you believe to be true about your client's problems, why they're struggling, and what they really need to succeed. You'll differentiate your offers and build a following of like-minded people.

3. Be social on social media. Too often, we post like we're shouting at a crowd through a megaphone. But communication goes two ways. Invite conversations, ask questions, answer questions, and encourage interaction by interacting. Don't just "post and ghost" without replying to comments. I should also note that posts showing your face get far more engagement. So get your face out there. People want to see you!

4. Show the inside story and give behind-the-scenes looks into your business, so it's not just about what you sell, but how you do the work. These types of posts connect really well. Think office tour videos and posts that give insights into your process. You don't have to wait until your desk is tidy and your hair is done.

5. When you are being transparent in ways other businesses in your niche typically aren't, say so. You don't have to name names, but if there is a dominant trope in your

field, call it out when you do the opposite. This creates awareness that the dominant trope is a problem and highlights your conscious choice to do things differently, earning the trust of your audience.
6. Don't just sell: Inform and engage. Just like with a newsletter, don't just make a post when you have something to sell. Offer value and connection for about two-thirds of your content, with offers making up the last third. I write informative and/or point of view posts, share personal stories for connection posts, and round it out with posts promoting paid offers. At least until I'm launching something new—for the launch, every post is about the offer, though I weave in value and connection at the same time.
7. Share the love: Use your platform to promote other people, products, services, businesses, and books you believe in. You can create ecosystems of mutual support this way because the people you feature today just might feature you when you're launching a new offer tomorrow.

When you consciously use social media to challenge damaging norms, to preach your point of view, and meaningfully connect with your audience, it becomes a healthy energetic exchange. It can be interactive, rather than extractive. And I believe we can use it to change our culture for the better.

Takeaways

1. **Curate your feed with intention:** Ruthlessly eliminate content that contradicts your values or harms your mental health. Follow accounts that inspire, inform, and expand your perspective. Your feed can either tear you down or build you up—choose wisely.
2. **Use social media's ability to influence for good:** Social media is inherently designed to influence. Channel this power to reinforce positive values, challenge harmful narratives, and inspire authentic connection.
3. **Turn rage into resonance:** When content from others sparks a reaction, use it as creative fuel. Trace the values at the root of your response and create content that embodies the opposite—aligned with your ethics and audience's needs.
4. **Be transparent, not aspirationally misleading:** Avoid selling a dream that's unattainable for most. Share realistic results, acknowledge privilege, and offer actionable insights to build trust and connection.
5. **Balance honesty with inspiration:** Your audience craves authenticity. Show the messy, imperfect reality instead of a polished façade, and balance inspiring content with transparent, actionable advice.
6. **Engage, don't just broadcast:** Social media isn't a one-way street. Foster dialogue by responding to comments, asking questions, and creating interactive content. Be present and personable.
7. **Lead by example:** Highlight how your ethical approach to social media marketing differs from the norm. Be explicit about your commitment to honesty and empowerment and invite others to do the same.

CHAPTER 10

Conscious Word Choice

I do not practice word policing. I will never tell you that you can, can't, should, or shouldn't use a word or phrase. I won't even judge you silently if you use a word or phrase that I don't choose to use myself (unless it's "utilize," "imagine," or "strive." I react to those words the way some people react to the word "moist"—*shudder*). There's been a growing trend to try and control everyone's language online. Some of it is for the good, and some of it is...well, it's a slippery slope to Orwellian double-speak or a politically correct dystopia where the punishment for saying the wrong thing or something in the wrong way gets you ostracized from polite society.

Unpopular opinion: I think good intentions are worth something. I think educating yourself is worth more. And I think punishing well-intentioned people with censure instead of gentle education is worthless. If you disagree, I'm not going to fight about it. Your reasons are valid.

Frustratingly, the list of words you "should" and shouldn't use changes every five minutes, so even with the best intentions, it's easy to get left behind in the diction wars. The word "queer," for example, has seen both sides—once extremely offensive and now reclaimed by the LGBTQIA+ community (an acronym that also has its issues: some consider it offensive because it lumps a lot of unique identities together instead of giving them individual respect, while others defend it as an inclusive term that acknowledges diversity).[48]

I won't give you an exhaustive list of potentially offensive words here because this book would be instantly obsolete. But I will give you a framework of questions to ask yourself when choosing which words to use when writing for your business to minimize harm to others and risk to yourself.

How to define your own naughty list

Are you scratching your head, thinking, "What words are you talking about?" Here are a few I frequently come across that are worthy of careful consideration:
1. Tribe—cultural appropriation
2. Spirit animal—cultural appropriation
3. Blind spot—ableist
4. Crippling—ableist
5. Dark side (or labeling something negative as "dark" or "black")—racist

For many words, there are arguments in favor of using them (*but there were tribes in Israel!*) and arguments against (*it's cultural appropriation!*). If you're unsure if a word might be offensive, look it up.[49] And then make your decision once you have all of the information.

I am not saying you can only use words that no one, anywhere, finds offensive. It would be incredibly difficult to communicate (and

---

[48] The University of California San Francisco has an excellent LGBTQIA+ glossary page. https://lgbtq.ucsf.edu/glossary-terms

[49] Recommended resources: *The Conscious Style Guide* by Karin Yin and its website https://consciousstyleguide.com/ and the antiracist language guide from the University of Arizona https://lib.arizona.edu/employees/anti-racist-guide

communication is hard enough already). I am arguing in favor of conscious, informed word choice.

One of my clients chose not to use the word "shaman" on her website or in her marketing even though she was, in fact, formally trained in shamanic practices and descended from the Sámi people who have a shamanic tradition. (Sámi use the word "noaidi" for shaman.) She was concerned about the appearance of cultural appropriation. Could she have defended her use of the word? I think so. Did she want to open that can of worms whenever she posted on social media? No. And "witchy/intuitive" worked for her equally well.

Questions to ask yourself when choosing which words to use:
- If I use this word, will it hurt someone?
- If I use this word, will it help someone?
- Am I afraid to use this word because of what other people will say or think? Should I be?
- Where did this word come from? Does it have a history of harm?
- Where did this word come from? Does it belong to a culture or spiritual tradition that is not mine?
- Am I profiting off this word from a place of privilege when other people who've used this word were punished or oppressed?
- Has there been backlash about this word? Do I want to invite that into my life if I use it?

Violence in marketing language

Another area where I see problematic words is in the language used to describe marketing. In fact, the language of copywriting and marketing tactics is shockingly violent when you examine it closely.

- Should you use "tripwire" offers (low-cost offers that are an easy yes because they require very little commitment of time or money, but the psychological underpinning is that any "yes" makes a future "yes" more likely, even for a higher-ticket offer)? "Tripwire" is a word that comes from tripping over a wire that triggers a bomb. Not the best origin story.
- Should you use "bleeding-neck" problems that are so incredibly painful and urgent that people will do anything to stop the hemorrhage?
- Should you be on the "cutting edge" or "bleeding edge" of marketing practices? Does everything have to be so bloody?
- Should you call people "prospects" or "leads" when they are, in fact, humans who are so much more than your ideal client avatar?
- Should your goal in copywriting be "conversions"—with all of those religious and cult-like implications? And even if you use the marketing definition that "a conversion happens any time a user does what you want them to do"—do you want to call your clients "users" like you're a drug dealer?
- Should you aim for "persuasive" or "compelling" or "irresistible" copy? Is persuading or compelling people something you want to do or is it too close to coercion? Shouldn't people be able to resist? Maybe you just want to clearly say what you're doing and encourage the reader to decide if it's what they need—without persuading like a politician or compelling like a vampire.

Some of these words make me cringe, and I will not use them. Some are just useful and there isn't a better word out there (which is why I still use lead and prospect or prospective client because the alternatives are so wordy). I will never be the word police. I just want you to keep an ear out for what makes you uncomfortable because it probably should.

How to respond to criticism with integrity

If you're really on the ball, you've probably found problematic words and phrases in this book already. I apologize. We only know what we know, and so much of our awareness is determined by our social circles, socioeconomic status, race, and privilege. But I commit to constantly learning and consciously improving to avoid doing harm, and I will try not to offer any excuses for my ignorance.

And that's how you apologize if you mess up.
Apologize sincerely.
Acknowledge the harm you caused.
Commit to doing better.
Don't offer excuses for your ignorance.

And definitely don't ask the aggrieved party to explain why they're offended or ask them to educate you on issues you are perfectly capable of googling yourself. Marginalized people have enough to do without educating the rest of us (it's an absurd amount of unpaid emotional and intellectual labor).

But if you're facing minor criticism that you feel is valid, it might make sense to just quietly change the word without making a big deal of it. Or, in some cases, opening a dialogue can be a welcome way to expand everyone's understanding. To be clear: I'm not talking about handling trolls. Trolls don't deserve your time or attention unless you find entertainment in baiting them. But reasonable people with reasonable concerns should be met with respect and care.

Choose your words wisely. Treat people kindly. It works most of the time.

What you absolutely should not do is allow your anxiety about being judged, censored, criticized, or ostracized to prevent you from writing anything at all. Sadly, I know some entrepreneurs who suffer from so much fear about what other people will say or think that they don't promote their businesses or engage on social channels, limiting their growth, income, and capacity to spread much-needed good in the world.

 *Words have power, and they can hurt. Just do your best, think carefully about how you write (not just what you write), apologize when you mess up, and do better next time.*

What words in your business do you use automatically? Take a moment to reflect—are they the best fit for your values?

Takeaways

1. **Ask critical questions:** When choosing words, reflect on their impact and origin. Consider whether they carry harmful histories or cultural appropriation.
2. **Balance awareness with courage:** Be mindful of evolving language sensitivities, but don't silence yourself because of fear of judgment. Words matter, but anxiety over perfection can stifle meaningful communication.
3. **Question whether you want to use violent marketing language:** Evaluate common marketing terms like "tripwire," "cutting edge," or "bleeding-neck." Decide if they align with your values or veer too close to manipulation or violence.
4. **Embrace nuance:** Some problematic words lack alternatives that are clear and succinct. If you can't find a better alternative, use these words consciously and be prepared to adapt as language and understanding evolve.
5. **Learn and improve:** Mistakes are inevitable. Commit to learning from them and apologizing when needed without getting defensive (that's the hard part).
6. **Bookmark trusted resources to check word trends:** University websites are often the most up to speed and I've included some in the resources section.
7. **When in doubt, test your content:** Show your post, content, or website copy to a small, trusted audience with diverse backgrounds and ask them what they think.

CHAPTER 11

AI Copy—Yes, No, It Depends?

By now, you know my shameful secret: I'm a writer who doesn't enjoy writing. Content marketing for my business is a chore (except for my newsletter, which I do genuinely enjoy). My policy is: If I don't like doing it, outsource it if possible! AI, like ChatGPT and Claude. ai, are so tempting to turn to when I need to congeal scattered ideas into a blog post or divide an already written blog post into social media posts. But, like most temptations, the easy way comes with consequences you might not want to pay. In this chapter, we'll explore whether you want to use AI to help with your copy, and if you do, how to do it as ethically as possible.

As an experiment, I asked ChatGPT if it knew what ethical marketing is. Yes, yes it does.

> ### Query: "Do you know what ethical marketing is?"
>
> CHATGPT SAID:
>
> Yes, ethical marketing is an approach that prioritizes honesty, fairness, and responsibility in the way products and services are promoted to consumers. It involves aligning marketing strategies with moral principles and values, ensuring that all promotional activities are transparent, truthful, and respectful to the audience.

KEY PRINCIPLES OF ETHICAL MARKETING

1. **Honesty and Transparency:**
   - Ethical marketing avoids misleading claims, exaggerations, or false promises. It ensures that all information provided is accurate and that any limitations or risks associated with a product or service are clearly communicated.
2. **Respect for Consumers:**
   - This approach values the rights and dignity of consumers, avoiding manipulative tactics or exploiting vulnerabilities. It emphasizes understanding and addressing the genuine needs and concerns of the target audience.
3. **Fairness:**
   - Ethical marketing ensures that all customers are treated fairly, without discrimination or bias. This includes fair pricing, clear terms and conditions, and responsible handling of customer data.
4. **Social Responsibility:**
   - Companies practicing ethical marketing often consider the broader impact of their actions on society and the environment. They may engage in sustainable practices, support social causes, and avoid promoting harmful products.
5. **Integrity:**
   - Maintaining a consistent ethical stance across all marketing efforts builds long-term trust and loyalty with customers. This includes owning up to mistakes and being willing to make amends when necessary.

6. **Consumer Education:**
   - Ethical marketing involves educating consumers, providing them with the information they need to make informed decisions. This can involve clear product labeling, honest advertising, and transparent business practices.

WHY ETHICAL MARKETING MATTERS:

- **Builds Trust:** Ethical marketing fosters trust between a brand and its customers, leading to stronger relationships and brand loyalty.
- **Enhances Reputation:** Companies known for their ethical practices often enjoy a better reputation, attracting customers who value integrity and social responsibility.
- **Reduces Legal Risks:** By adhering to ethical standards, companies reduce the risk of legal issues related to false advertising, unfair practices, or consumer rights violations.
- **Promotes Long-Term Success:** Ethical marketing strategies contribute to sustainable business growth, as they prioritize the long-term well-being of both the company and its customers.

Ethical marketing is not just about following the law but about doing what is right for customers, society, and the environment. It requires a commitment to transparency, fairness, and social responsibility, ensuring that marketing efforts contribute positively to the world.

I think ChatGPT did a great job with this definition. But...

Is AI an ethical tool for writing your copy—or anything else?

The quick answer: Not right now, but probably not for the reasons you think.

The longer answer: The most pressing issue I see with AI, though not the only one, is its environmental impact.

A report by Goldman Sachs found that a ChatGPT query uses nearly 10 times more electricity than a Google search query[50]—and with AI becoming a non-optional addition to many search results pages, this impact is poised to be significant. The International Energy Agency found that "energy consumption by global data centres [for AI] could more than double by 2026, 'reaching levels that exceed large nations.'"[51] The issue isn't just about energy, it's also about water use and electronic waste. In a research collaboration between *The Washington Post* and the University of California Riverside, they found that ChatGPT-4 consumes just over one bottle of water to write a 100-word email. And these data centers produce electronic waste containing chemicals that contaminate soil, water, and air.

Right now, you're contributing to global warming with every query. Although, as the technology evolves, it also has the potential to solve environmental problems. It's not completely black and white.

---

[50] "AI is poised to drive 160% increase in data center power demand," Goldman Sachs, May 14, 2024. https://www.goldmansachs.com/insights/articles/AI-poised-to-drive-160-increase-in-power-demand
[51] "California wildfires raise alarm on water-guzzling AI like ChatGPT," Fortune, January 9, 2025

Other ethical considerations are:
- AI works based on gleaning ideas, writing and art from unpaid, uncredited writers and artists, essentially stealing work it repackages as its own.
- AI has a history of reflecting and amplifying biases, including racism and sexism, that exists in its creators, training, and source material.
- AI can hallucinate facts, numbers, and advice based on what it "thinks" you want to hear. It can make up results and studies that don't exist, it can make up statistics that support your theory, and it can get answers wrong.
- AI has trouble discriminating between good sources and bad sources of information. Kind of like your uncle who sends you "news articles" from the *Weekly World News* and swears Elvis is alive and well in Gilroy, the garlic capital of California.

That said, AI isn't going away. And you may not have a choice to use it since major search engines, meeting software, and smartphones are rolling out more and more AI features that you can't turn off. What we need is uncompromising environmental legislation. But until we get it, it's your call. Personally, I don't think we can afford to ignore AI, pretend it isn't there, or refuse to learn how to use it because it's the future. I also, perhaps optimistically, believe efficiency and environmental policy will improve…eventually.

So how do you use AI responsibly and effectively for your copy (if you choose to use it)?

First and foremost: Minimize the number of queries it takes to get the result you need by learning to write better queries in the first place. This alone will reduce your environmental impact.

How to write better queries

The more specific and detailed you can be with your queries, the higher quality answers you'll receive. Think of AI as a smart college intern who can follow directions pretty well but might go off the rails at any time.

A query structure I've found useful is:
1. Tell AI what or who's perspective to write from. Yours? Describe who you are and what you do. Include your point of view on your approach and why you find it works better.
2. Describe your ideal client—who they are, what they want, what they struggle with, what fears they have, and what they hope to be able to do. This requires you to know your audience really well. AI can't do this work for you.
3. Describe the job you need it to do and the effect you'd like the copy to have (i.e., I need a sales page for X offer and I would like the reader to feel uplifted, inspired, and validated).
4. Feed it your own written material from earlier drafts, past emails, or blog posts, and tell AI to incorporate your style into the result (you can also ask it to analyze your style).
5. Use AI to develop a custom style guide explaining your brand voice, your values, words you use often, and the tone you like to use—friendly, professional, warm and welcoming, funny, irreverent, satirical, etc. Then feed that style guide back to AI every time you give it a new query.
6. Add any other parameters, like word count, or areas of focus.

EXAMPLE QUERY:

> "Hello, today you are an ethical copywriter for service-based entrepreneurs who are often life coaches, spiritual coaches, healers, and therapists. They struggle to clearly articulate what they do and why their approach works better than other things their clients have tried, and they want to talk about what they do honestly and transparently, without manipulative sales tactics. You are writing a newsletter, using the same style as if you're writing to a dear friend (informal, warm tone) to announce your new book on ethical copywriting. I will paste the synopsis of the book below. Please pay special attention to crafting an entertaining, engaging opening paragraph that highlights how much easier and more fun it is to run a business ethically because ethical marketing attracts better-fit clients and there is no dissonance between your values and actions. Please limit the word count to under 300 words."

This is the first result I got, and some of it is really good and some of it makes me cringe. That's par for the course.

Subject Line: Selling with Soul: My New Book on Ethical Copywriting

Hey [First Name],

Have you ever had that moment where your business finally *feels right*? [NOTE: Opening with a question is an extremely common copywriting trope that I consciously avoid because it's overused—but AI uses it precisely because it's used often!] The clients are the perfect fit—they get you, they're a joy to work with, and you don't have to bend yourself into a pretzel to make the sale. Plus, there's no icky feeling in the pit of your stomach because your marketing aligns with your values. It's like slipping into your favorite cozy sweater: comfortable, effortless, and *you*. That's the magic of running a business ethically—and the heart of my new book, *[Title Here]*.

For years, I wrestled with why some copywriting tactics made me cringe, even if they technically "worked." Pain points, countdown timers, manufactured urgency—sure, they convert, but at what cost? Eventually, I realized the answer: they're designed to manipulate, not serve.

So, I tore it all down and started fresh. This book is the result. Inside, you'll find my favorite swaps for those pushy techniques, a step-by-step guide to writing generous, story-driven copy, and (my favorite part!) tools to help you question every marketing strategy until it aligns with *your* values.

Because here's the thing: ethical marketing isn't just about selling stuff without guilt. It's about building a business that feels like home—for you *and* your clients. And that's when running a business becomes not only easier but way more fun.

I can't wait for you to dive in. The book is coming soon, but if you want a sneak peek or first dibs, hit reply and let me know.

With love and high vibes, [Ugh, I would never say "high vibes"!]

[Your Name]

P.S. Get ready to expand the conversation about marketing. We're doing this together. ♥ [Cutesy emojis are so overdone]

It's a decent draft, mostly accurate, and copies my tone well, but it's not something I'd be comfortable sending as-is. At this stage, you can give feedback and ask AI to come up with another draft, but that's another bottle of water. What I do instead is take the rough draft and edit it to remove the cringe bits, check for accuracy, and infuse my personality. You'll reach your final draft stage much faster than if you started with a blank page.

Notice that I am only feeding AI my own copy to draw from rather than asking it to come up with ideas and words on its own. The results are much better and more likely to sound like me, it's an ethical move to only use your own work, and it also helps prevent one of the dangers of using AI: derivative copy.

The dangers of derivative AI copy

"Derivative" means to imitate the work of someone else, and that is exactly what AI is designed to do: Imitate, assimilate, and synthesize. AI works by gathering ideas that already exist on the internet, taking the ones used most often, and smushing them together in different combinations. The result? Derivative copy that sounds like everyone else because it was created from everyone else.

Because of this crowdsourcing, derivative copy can reproduce the biases and discrimination found in its sources, which means subtly biased words and ideas based on race, gender, or political leanings sneak into your copy. These can be especially hard to spot if you're on the privileged side of those conversations and haven't developed sensitivity to them.

One interesting example of how bias—sexism and racism, specifically—is embedded within AI was with an experiment done with virtual robots programmed with popular AI algorithms. The task was to scan blocks with people's faces and identify the faces with different words, like "criminal," "janitor," and "homemaker." For "criminal," the robots repeatedly chose a Black man's face. For "janitor" and "homemaker," it was a toss-up between women and people of color.[52]

The way bias shows up in AI copy can be sneaky.

I conducted an experiment of my own using ChatGPT to write advertising copy for a vacuum cleaner. Here's what happened.

My query, which I deliberately left gender neutral:
> "Can you create story-driven marketing copy of no more than 100 words to sell a vacuum cleaner to a homeowner? Tell me a little about who that homeowner is and what they care about and how a good vacuum can improve their day."

ChatGPT said:

Marketing Copy:

Your living room tells the story of life well-lived—movie nights, kids' snacks, and furry friends. But the mess? Not so great. Meet the [Vacuum Name], your secret weapon for a spotless home in minutes. With powerful suction and whisper-quiet tech, it tackles crumbs, pet hair, and dust like a pro—so you can focus on what really matters: game night, snuggles, and making memories. Because a clean home shouldn't steal your time; it should set the stage for your life.

This taps into emotional benefits (time-saving, family moments) while highlighting practical features.

I couldn't immediately spot any bias. In fact, it seemed perfectly

---

[52] Hundt, Andrew, et al. "Robots Enact Malignant Stereotypes." *Proceedings of the 2022 ACM Conference on Fairness, Accountability, and Transparency (FAccT)*, Association for Computing Machinery, 2022, https://doi.org/10.1145/3531146.3533138.

gender neutral to me. So I asked a follow-up question—one that was, admittedly, loaded.

"Do you think this ad's target audience is male or female?"

ChatGPT's response:
> The ad's target audience skews female, given its focus on family moments, nurturing spaces, and managing a clean home while balancing life. These themes often align with marketing stereotypes that associate household tasks and emotional labor with women, especially in traditional advertising.
>
> That said, this copy could appeal to any homeowner who values family time and a clean, comfortable home. If you'd like to make the ad more gender-neutral or intentionally target men, we could adjust the language to emphasize efficiency, ease of use, and time-saving benefits without leaning as much into family-oriented imagery. Would you like me to tweak it?

Not only did ChatGPT point out that the copy did, in fact, "skew female" for reasons I'd completely overlooked (being female, I was too close to see it), it offered gender-neutral alternatives. AI may be as biased as the rest of us (because it's based on us), but just like examining our own biases, sometimes we just have to ask the right questions.

Embedded bias aside, there's another ethical issue associated with derivative copy: grabbing words, phrases, and ideas from others who did not give consent and are not given credit.

In the words of Wallace Notestein, a professor of English history at Yale University in 1929, "If you copy from one book, that's plagiarism; if you copy from many books, that's research." But, as academics will enthusiastically point out, research requires citations. I would love to see AI use citations. Just imagine if you not only got the answer to your query but a source list with recommended reading? Or a list of artists used to generate that "pop-art inspired picture of a tabby cat eating tomato soup" that you could look up and learn about? Even better if AI companies paid artists!

AI is a terrible research assistant but an excellent translator

While writing this book I've searched for a lot of studies and the AI-generated responses at the top of the search engine results pages have been helpful—until I learned it was literally making up research. I was searching for statistics on newsletter follower conversions compared with social media follower conversions for Chapter 8, and I was thrilled to find this statement, courtesy of Google's AI:

"According to available data, newsletter followers are significantly more likely to make a purchase compared to social media followers, with studies showing that email subscribers can be up to 10 times more likely to convert into customers than social media followers, indicating a much higher potential for sales when engaging with an email list."

I searched everywhere for the origin of this data. I paid my VA to continue searching for the data. I really wanted this data! *It doesn't exist.* But I learned a valuable lesson: AI's confirmation bias means it tends to seek and interpret information that supports the outcome you want, rather than dispassionately evaluating the evidence and delivering a conclusion. In the words of Sherlock Holmes, "It is a capital mistake to theorize before one has data. Insensibly one begins to twist facts to suit theories, instead of theories to suit facts."

You can find better research assistants, but when it comes to translating complex, esoteric, or just plain scattered ideas into simple language, AI is an incredible tool. My clients range from mystics to poets to academics, and between them, the language they use to describe their modalities can be…opaque, to say the least. On occasion, I feed my raw notes from client interviews through AI so it can sift through the verbiage and explain it to me like I'm a precocious six-year-old.[53] If you've found that the language you use to describe your modalities confuses people, see what happens when AI translates it for you.

The "explain it to me" query structure:
1. Tell AI who your ideal clients are and what they need for background.
2. Present the context for how this copy will be read, like "I need a 100-character summary of what I do and how it helps people for my Instagram bio."
3. Ask AI to simplify, or explain simply, what you do, including only the most important details. For example, "Simplify these notes for an audience unfamiliar with these modalities, focusing on the benefits rather than definitions of the modalities."
4. Give AI a hint as to the tone you prefer (casual, friendly, conversational, and warm are my favorites).
5. Paste your long, esoteric, poetic, and potentially confusing draft into AI and hit enter.

I used this process to go from raw notes like this…

---

[53] In my defense, I graduated with honors, summa cum laude, with an English major from UCLA. My reading comprehension is above average, and I am particularly good at analyzing poetry. That said, sometimes, my clients' descriptions of what they do can still make my eyes cross.

My client is creating in the world and would benefit from recharging to keep things manifesting in alignment with their heart vision. My client needs support to learn to ground and co-create in the physical. Struggling in the world as an intuitive person, perhaps with a history of trauma, with a desire to move beyond surviving in life to thriving with inner strength and tenderness toward self. What is missing from mainstream approaches is ignoring the vision and wisdom of helping spirits. As humans, we have a limited view of our problems and solutions. But partnering with helping spirits helps you get the higher perspective to create shifts in your life, starting at the energetic level.

To a sales page opener like this, which I was able to write after AI translated two full pages of notes into simpler language:

Integration Journey Circle for Self-Care, Guidance, & Healing

A safe space to ground, recharge, and deepen your spiritual connection with others on the same path.

You've done the work to open the door to the spirit world. Now, it's time to integrate those experiences, tend to your soul's needs, and nourish yourself deeply—body, mind, and spirit.

If you've been feeling overwhelmed, disconnected, or stuck in familiar patterns, this circle is your refuge. It's where you'll find guidance, support, and the energy to keep showing up in your life and sharing your gifts with the world.

You can see why, even with the costs, AI is a tool worth getting to know. It has so much potential for good, though I also cannot ignore the potential for harm.

Here are my dos and don'ts for using AI, as ethically as possible, to speed up your writing process without sacrificing quality.

AI Dos

DO: Use it to brainstorm ideas for blog posts, newsletters, email subject lines, and social media posts. You will likely reject almost all the ideas it presents, but it will spur your brain into getting creative.

DO: Use AI to analyze other people's writing that you like. It's AMAZING at dissecting sales pages and emails and telling you exactly what is working and why.

For example, if you copy the entire text from any of my sales pages, paste it into AI, and ask, "Please diagram this sales page and tell me what each section is doing and why it works," you will get a comprehensive lesson in how to write sales pages *my way*. Try it! The caveat: If you feed AI a sales page that isn't effective, it will tell you why it's great anyway because that is what you asked. It's not good at critical thinking.

DO: Use AI to analyze your own writing and tell you about your unique voice and style, and what parts of your writing are most effective and least effective. It can provide useful insights.

AI Don'ts

DON'T: Don't use AI to write for you. It's tempting, I know. But even when you painstakingly train AI to write in your brand voice (which can be done), it's still potentially grabbing information from other people on the internet unless you deliberately only feed it your work. Even then, if you don't put your spin on the content, it will sound stale and stuffy. Your clients (and potential clients) want your unique life experience, expertise, and fresh perspective. Your blog, social media, and newsletters should be where you shine, and you can't outsource that to AI.

DON'T: Don't use AI-generated art for your website, Instagram, blog posts, or anything business-related or public-facing. It is stealing art from real artists without giving credit or payment, which is bad in itself, but you also don't know how that will legally play out in the future. Ethically, it's a clear no-go (just pay an artist; websites like Creative Market make it easy). That said, I have used AI art for my amusement before I knew the eco-implications because I wanted to see a mini schnauzer in a trench coat solving crimes in Victorian London. When we know better, we do better, right?

Here are some other ways you can use AI to inspire your copywriting—but not to do the work for you. With each of these, be careful about which of AI's suggestions you incorporate because it will tell you what *most* marketers do and most marketers are not ethical!

1. **Feedback on your drafts** Paste your copy—for sales pages or emails—into AI, tell it your goals, and ask it to suggest improvements and point out any inconsistencies.
2. **Learn through examples** Ask AI to write sample sales copy for different products, services, or audiences. Analyzing these examples can help you understand different techniques and approaches.
3. **Practice rewriting** Paste in existing sales copy (yours or others) and ask for a rewrite or improvement. This can

help you see different ways to structure or phrase your messaging.
4. **Get ideas for hooks, headlines, and email subject lines** Ask AI for catchy headlines, hooks, or opening lines. You can then tweak these suggestions to suit your style and audience or throw them out because you've thought of something better (which is what I always end up doing).
5. **Identify buyer psychology triggers** Inquire about the psychology-based techniques behind someone else's sales copy or your own. AI can pinpoint where urgency, scarcity, social proof, and other triggers show up so you can consciously choose whether or not to use them.
6. **Grammar and clarity checks** Run your copy through AI for grammar, spelling, and clarity checks. AI can suggest ways to make your writing more concise; just make sure it doesn't end up sounding more like a textbook than a human.
7. **Brainstorming sessions** Use AI to brainstorm ideas for how your service might benefit your ideal client and objections your ideal client may have—then validate those ideas with your actual ideal clients and use their client language (i.e., what they say) over what AI tells you.

You don't have to use AI at all if it feels icky. It does take ideas, words, and art without giving credit or compensation to the originator—it's how the entire system operates. But I also think the human mind is a patchwork of other people's ideas we've heard, art we've seen, and creations we've experienced. Intelligence, human or otherwise, is taking ideas from different places and recombining them into new patterns we find more useful. There probably isn't a single original idea in this book or in the author's head. Every story has already been told, and I don't think we're wrong for finding new ways to tell them. I think it enriches the human experience.

For now, with the ethical considerations in mind, I choose to use AI sparingly.

Takeaways

1. **Be selective with how you use AI (*if* you use AI):** AI is helpful for idea generation, brainstorming, and grammar checks, but rely on your voice and insights for the final copy.
2. **Avoid full AI dependence:** Don't let AI write your copy from scratch. Instead, use it to create a rough draft or first-pass idea that you refine into something uniquely yours.
3. **Check for biases:** Review AI-generated content carefully to ensure it doesn't carry hidden biases, prejudices, or harmful language.
4. **Learn by analyzing:** Use AI to analyze sales pages and other content you admire, breaking down effective techniques to apply to your writing.
5. **Experiment with AI for short, pithy copy:** Ask AI for catchy headlines or subject lines and modify them to fit your style and resonate with your audience.
6. **Don't use AI instead of real client language:** Run queries to see how AI explains complex topics in simple terms, then cross-check that with how your clients describe what you do. Client language is almost always better (as long as it's clear and not too generic), but the clarity AI can achieve is helpful.

Conclusion

You might have found me out by now: There are many areas around ethics, marketing, and copywriting that I haven't definitively figured out. My opinions around AI, social media, or using positive reinforcement for email newsletters may change; writing them down already has me questioning them. But that is the reason for this book. To get you to question yourself and business "experts," as well as the dominant paradigms of extractive marketing practices. If you're questioning, you're doing it right.

Business coach Stephanie Wasylyk said it best: "I feel like once I found out about ethical marketing, nothing I do is ever 'ethical enough.' There's always better. And it's *paralyzing*." She then worried about using ableist language like "paralyzing," thus illustrating the spiral of self-censure. Can anything or anyone ever be ethical enough to avoid criticism?

Nope.

Dear reader, I don't want you to use this book to judge yourself, to rate yourself on a barometer of ethical enoughness, or to become too afraid to say or do anything in public because someone might call you out (or worse, cancel you). It is scary. The amount of judgment out there terrifies me. The lack of grace we give each other makes me grieve.

I think part of being a good business owner and good person is to try your best to do no harm, to acknowledge and apologize when you've done harm, to give other people the grace you'd appreciate in return, and to go forth and say, and do, with courage. Putting yourself out there is a daily act of bravery, especially when you're willing to assert where you draw the line.

Because the person next to you might disagree with your line. They might say, "No, you're a bad [person, business owner, marketer] if you draw the line there" or "drawing the line there doesn't work." Then you need the courage of your convictions to stick with the choice that feels right to you or possibly even more courage to reconsider where you could be doing better.

It takes courage to be an ethical copywriter when you see "everyone else" marketing the other way.

Ethical copywriting will not make or break your business in the short term. Other things will, like your understanding of your niche, how well your offers deliver what your clients need, how deep that desire or need is, and how well you can articulate why your offer is better than other solutions they've tried.

But, in the long term, when you commit to treating people well and delivering on your promises while holding your boundaries sacred—I can promise you that works. That leads to clients who trust you, buy from you, benefit from you, and come back with their friends. It is the path to sustainability.

It's also the path to running a business you absolutely love.

Resources

Books, Podcasts, People to Follow

BOOKS

- *Algorithms of Oppression: How Search Engines Reinforce Racism* by Safia Noble
- *Authentic Content Marketing, 3rd edition* by George Kao
- *Braiding Sweetgrass and The Serviceberry: Abundance and Reciprocity in the Natural World* by Robin Wall Kimmerer
- *It's Not (All) Your Fault: Self-help and the Individualization of Oppression* by Sharon Podobnik
- *Rest Is Resistance: A Manifesto* by Tricia Hersey
- *The Antiracist Business Book: An Equity Centered Approach to Work, Wealth, and Leadership* by Trudi Lebrón
- *The Conscious Style Guide* by Karin Yin
- *Tiny Beautiful Things: Advice on Love and Life from Dear Sugar* by Cheryl Strayed

PODCASTS

- DUPED with Dr. Michelle Mazur and Maggie Patterson
- Maintenance Phase with Michael Hobbes and Aubrey Gordon

VALUES-DRIVEN BUSINESS COACHES TO FOLLOW

- Caroline Leon
- Gemma Gilbert
- Maggie Gentry at Rest Day Creative
- Mark Silver at Heart of Business
- Dr. Michelle Mazur
- Rebecca Tracey at The Uncaged Life
- Tad Hargrave at Marketing for Hippies

SOCIAL MEDIA STRATEGY

- Andréa Jones at www.onlinedrea.com
- Strong Brand Social at www.strongbrandsocial.com
- Meg Casebolt at https://megcasebolt.com/

FURTHER READING:

- The antiracist language guide from the University of Arizona https://lib.arizona.edu/employees/anti-racist-guide
- The LGBTQIA+ glossary page from The University of California San Francisco https://lgbtq.ucsf.edu/glossary-terms

Gratitude

It takes a village to write a book.

Thank you, Stephanie Wasylyk, business coach for ADHD entrepreneurs, for saying, "The 500th man who wrote a book about marketing did not worry about whether someone else had written it first." Any time I worried, "Has someone else said this already? Did they say it better? Should I say this at all?" I came back to these words of wisdom. My business group of *Growth Besties*, of which Stephanie is a member, has been there for me the whole way with encouragement, suggestions, and insights. Rachael Cumberland-Dodd, Susan Doerksen Castro, and Laura Perkins, your wisdom grounds me.

Thank you, Dr. Michelle Mazur and Maggie Patterson, for the many episodes of the *DUPED* podcast I listened to while editing this book. You're putting ethical marketing (and awareness of unethical marketing) on the map.

My business wouldn't have evolved in quite the same way without Caroline Leon and Tad Hargrave as my guiding constellation of ethical business way-showers. Your ideas have embedded themselves in my soul and in my work, and I will never stop giving you credit.

And credit must also be given to the strong women I work with and for because you've given me the best proving ground for ethical marketing: teaching copywriting to the conscious, caring and committed students in your own ethical business programs.

Rebecca Tracey, your commitment to telling the real stories behind entrepreneurship heavily inspired my understanding of transparency in content and social media. Even though I think you could sell your program based on your lifestyle, you choose to sell based on the value your clients actually receive (and not just, as you've joked, because "no one wants to live in a van and rock climb!")

Gemma Gilbert, you manage to do what I thought was impossible—scale a business while maintaining work/life balance, never sacrificing the quality of service to your clients, and managing an unassisted pull-up. I admire how you show up on your best days and your worst days, set healthy boundaries, and always deliver.

When women work together to support each other, everything is possible. I am deeply grateful for these relationships.

And so much credit needs to go to my mother, who taught me to appreciate the moral clarity of black and white and to take a stand to defend the line, and to friends and teachers since then who taught me the critical nuances found in the gray areas and that my line is not everyone's line (nor should it be). Cynthia Ward, Ming Holden, Alicia Ostarello, and The Drunk Austen Book Club ladies—you've each expanded my mind and heart and shown me better ways to be.

Finally, I have to thank my husband for constantly being my cheerleader, my patron of the arts, and always my best friend. Loving you holds me to a higher standard every day.

Special thanks to Autumn Tompkins, The Grumpy Grammarian, for a developmental edit that took my ideas to task, challenged my assumptions, and made this book so much better than it would have been without you.

And my sincere gratitude to Get It Done Productions, LLC for edits, encouragement, and doing the heavy lifting of getting this book out into the world.

www.ingramcontent.com/pod-product-compliance
Lightning Source LLC
Chambersburg PA
CBHW020244010526
44107CB00002B/83